earth pledge

Promoting Sustainability Since 1991

Earth Pledge is an award-winning environmental leader. We assist government,
industry and communities by researching
and applying innovative technologies that
balance human and natural systems. Our
Initiatives demonstrate practical solutions
that inspire and facilitate a global transition to sustainability.

FutureFashion White Papers are part of the Earth Pledge Series on Sustainable Development.

Earth Pledge
122 East 38th Street, New York, NY 10016
Telephone (212) 725-6611
www.earthpledge.org

President: Theodore W. Kheel

Executive Director: Leslie Hoffman

Managing Director: Greg Loosvelt

Editor: Leslie Hoffman

Assistant Editors: Sari Bernstein, Chris Niles, Amy Rocha

Design: Kristen Kriger

Production: Valerie English, Ricky Ferrer: Pix Design

Printed in Lincoln Park, NJ, by Greg Barber Co. on 100% recycled paper, cover: 25% hemp and 75% post-consumer waste; text
pages: Cascade Enviro Text 100% post-consumer waste and
chlorine free, using environmentally responsible techniques.

First Edition, October 2007

ISBN 978-0-9675099-2-1

TABLE OF CONTENTS

SECTION I: THE REAL MEANING
OF FUTUREFASHION

SECTION 5: THE SCIENCE OF CHANGE

Introduction

Leslie Hoffman, Executive Director
Earth Pledge

On a recent trip to China, I was introduced first hand to the vertical supply chain—from farm fields to packaged garments ready for shipment to the U.S. I will never again look at clothing in quite the same way. This experience has reminded me of how disconnected we have become from what it takes to sustain our lives. The materials and processes that are used and the number of people whose work is required seems to become less transparent over time. Somehow, this lack of awareness becomes an excuse for not taking responsibility for the consequences. I believe that by reconnecting to the source of the goods we use, as well as to their final resting place, our own lives become more interesting and richer and it enables us to make better decisions. It is this curiosity that has driven my work at Earth Pledge across the industries that touch us: food, building, energy, waste, and fashion.

If you had told me 20 years ago that one day I would publish a book about fashion, I might have scoffed. As a lifelong builder and gardener, I am happiest when the dress-code calls for plain old jeans and a t-shirt: that's my typical uniform for "saving the world." With so much serious and hard work to be done, it seems unimportant to worry about what to wear.

But if there's one thing that the environment can teach you, it's that everything is connected. In very different ways, Earth Pledge's other initiatives—Green Roofs, Farm to Table and Waste=Fuel—apply agricultural technology and expertise to the urban lifestyle, for the benefit of people, business and nature. In 2004, Christo and Jeanne-Claude's Gates Project for Central Park got us thinking about textiles, where they come from and where they go, and soon I found myself back on familiar territory: looking into the production, use and waste cycle that our apparel and interior furnishings create.

I quickly realized it is never silly to worry about what you wear. Many of the same unintended consequences that accompany construction or eating well also result from looking good. Textile and clothing manufacture typically entails significant water and petroleum use, fertilizer and pesticide spraying, affecting millions of people worldwide. Used apparel and industry refuse is dumped into our landfills at an alarming rate.

At Earth Pledge, we believe that it should be possible to enjoy a fashionable and sustainable lifestyle. In February of 2005, Earth Pledge and 28 leading fashion designers proved this with a runway show of sustainable fashion held during New York Fashion Week. The tremendous response generated by this landmark event demonstrated the need to connect designers with greener, smarter materials, processes and technologies and also to give them fresh visibility and branding opportunities. Recognizing the opportunity to have positive influence in the industry, we launched the FutureFashion Initiative and since then have built up a collection of eco-textiles, produced more fashion shows and lectured at top design schools.

It is a truism that what you wear says something about you. All of the contributors to this book believe that what you buy and what you make does too. You will find writings from a diverse and international group of scientists, manufacturers, entrepreneurs and designers who discuss topics ranging from organic fiber production to safer dyeing and finishing techniques, to broader issues of apparel consumption and disposal. As complex as fashion is, all of these authors offer a simple message: we need to look beyond the clothes on our back to consider the impact of their creation.

Preface

Diane von Furstenberg, President; Council of Fashion Designers of America, Designer

FutureFashion White Papers is an exploration that signifies movement towards a more sustainable fashion industry. It is an opportunity for me, as President of the Council of Fashion Designers of America (CFDA) and as a designer, to think about and evaluate the fashion industry as it stands today and to consider it evolving to become more environmentally friendly in the future. Since 2005, when I participated in Earth Pledge's FutureFashion runway show, the volume of environmental buzz has increased dramatically. It is now time for the fashion industry to weigh-in on this green discussion.

One of the CFDA's main roles is to support American designers both fiscally, through the CFDA/Vogue Fashion Fund, and creatively, which in turn benefits not only the fashion trade but public reception as well. While creative support certainly fosters new trends, fashion can't escape its contextual influences. There is no question that a global outcry for a more eco-conscientious society has filtered into the fashion industry. The demand for organic cotton has grown by 300 percent, and the number of clothing brands using organic materials has increased by 150 percent over the last three years. International interest in, and increasing demand for, environmental improvement and controls have changed textile production, clothing manufacturing, packaging and transportation standards. Everyday there are new technological advances to reduce textiles' environmental impact. This is an exceptional occasion; we can not only learn about these developments abstractly but should implement them as well.

The CFDA works to keep fashion at a high standard of cultural, artistic and modern relevance and we must also explore new sustainability standards. Our priority is to fulfill designers' need for creative independence and access to unique and luxury materials, and to begin to understand and work with those that are sustainable.

The CFDA is pleased to support Earth Pledge to educate designers on green material processing and clothing manufacturing through venues such as conferences, publications, fashion shows, and fabric exhibits. Earth Pledge's sustainable materials library is also a welcomed resource to the design community. From couture to mass-production, all price-points can make improvements in their carbon output while maintaining their artistic freedom. I agree with Earth Pledge; I do believe that style and sustainability can coexist.

I am committed to supporting American designers in their creative expression and to helping them lead a promising and profitable fashion industry. So much of fashion is inspired by nature and in turn, we must respect its delicacy. In this instance, the environment needs to be protected for its inherent relevance to fashion design, in addition to its and our own survival.

SECTION I:

THE REAL MEANING
OF FUTUREFASHION

The New Cool

Julie Gilhart, Senior Vice President, Fashion Director; Barneys New York

Barneys New York
575 Fifth Avenue
New York, NY 10017
www.barneys.com

Taste. Luxury. Humor. This is the company mantra at Barneys New York. Though it has withstood the test of time, an interesting thing has happened. The interpretation of the words is changing. Taste used to mean good style. Now taste is increasingly about making good, ethical choices. Luxury was about buying something extravagant. Now luxury is about making sure the extravagance is sustainable. Humor was about being cheeky. Now humor is about finding genuine laughter and lightness within a crisis.

Clearly, this value shift is a response to world events. In a sense, luxury fashion is just a reflection of the times. The best designers respond to the cultural mood aesthetically. That said, it is one of the paradoxes of this business that fashion has an awkward relationship to what goes on in the rest of the world. While fashion might—however abstractly—represent issues, it does not often engage directly with them, perhaps in the interest of maintaining or asserting artistic independence. For a long time, in relatively small yet influential circles, the discussion has expressed dissatisfaction with this situation.

There is a growing belief that creating beauty and preserving culture can contribute to—or at least not impede—making the world a better place. For some time, I have sensed the moment when the consumer would equate style with social and environmental consciousness and embrace ethical sustainability and organic principles, and that moment has finally arrived. Barneys New York is one of the few luxury fashion leaders to encourage the introduction of ethical and environmental issues into the business. Being personally sympathetic to the organic and green movements, and the Fashion Director for Barneys New York, nothing could excite me more than to participate in this change.

Barneys' unique challenge is maintaining the highest standards of style while starting to nurture a more practical application of ethical principles. Barneys comprises six flagship stores—in New York, Los Angeles, Chicago, Boston, Dallas and San Francisco—as well as fifteen CO-OP stores, which sell more casual clothing. In the next few years, Barneys will add more stores to its roster. Barneys New York is known as a "high-end specialty store," distinguished from a department store by the amount of high-style fashion luxury goods sold. Barneys has a reputation for celebrating and developing the new. The avant-garde doesn't frighten us, nor does merchandise steeped in tradition. We embrace great product. The store stands for style and quality, not mass and hype. The Barneys customer has a very high income and is fashion savvy. We serve an intelligent shopper who, more than anything, wants quality, distinction and style.

In my role at Barneys New York, I search for new resources and work closely with designers to support their creativity. I help develop interesting collaborations and communicate trends to the merchants, our stores and the press. I also work closely with the marketing, publicity, advertising and visual departments to develop concepts that advance the Barneys New York brand globally. In a sense, my job is to interface with anyone who drives or cultivates fashion.

The last ten years of fashion have been propelled and inspired by highly marketed, celebrity-driven luxury brands. This trend is beginning to feel outdated. The consumer is developing a taste for great product with ethical principles. Many people want to contribute to solving the global crisis that is occurring to our environment, but feel paralyzed as to what they can do. By applying their values to the products that they purchase, they feel empowered to contribute. It is a beautiful equation to tap into: satisfying the needs of the consumer, and providing products that sustain the environment.

Over the years, Barneys has looked into many eco-brands. But to be at Barneys, a brand has to be able to hold its own—among merchandise from the greatest designers in the world. Many eco-brands simply have not had the dynamic style quotient needed to compete. In the past, we have carried products from t-shirts to accessories that were eco-friendly—we just didn't advertise them as such. This is where the great shift is happening. Now it is "cool" to buy these kinds of products. Socially conscious ethical consumerism is The New Cool. Now we let the customer know when a brand has made ethical choices.

This is not to downplay the truism that what makes an eco-brand sell is still first and foremost style and quality. The item has to be alluring and have sex appeal. The fact that the product is manufactured responsibly adds value. Customers are not going to buy something just because it is eco-friendly. It has to look great, fit properly, feel luxurious and be stylish. If a brand can accomplish all that, then it has huge potential.

Seeing the opportunity, many mainstream fashion designers are willing to explore organic and sustainable principles, but their path is littered with obstacles. Researching new materials, dyes and supply chains takes effort and frequently increases the costs to the design exercise. Additional costs are just what designers are trying desperately to avoid. They often feel overwhelmed with the business side of fashion as it is. Very few feel that they have enough time to concentrate on design—the reason they chose their vocation in the first place.

Where it can, Barneys tries to support designers who are looking for ways to incorporate organic and sustainable principles into their businesses. However, I believe that there is a need for initiatives (perhaps even nonprofit-led) that provide information on where designers can go to find raw materials and fabrics that are aesthetically competitive and of high quality, as well as to discover factories that adhere to sustainable business practices. On the other side of the equation, retailers must endeavor to support the designers' efforts. The bottom line counts, and it takes a lot of courage to make choices that are more costly.

By 2006, Barneys New York felt ready to present our customer with a fashion product that educated about the viability of sustainable philosophies in a tangible way. We tapped the organic business model and fashion expertise of Loomstate to create a proprietary collection that is sexy, stylish, affordable and addresses The New Cool. It is a collaboration to build a collection that is beautiful as the quality of life it represents: healthy soil, where farm meets ocean, fashion and style from the inside out. The first collection included lightweight knit dresses and tops, watercolor washed graphics, soft terry hoodies and sexy denim shorts and skirts. We expect our very discriminating customers to be impressed, and hope they will savor the satisfaction that comes with buying things that are made well, look great and are backed by an ethical mission. The long-term goal of this project is to set up criteria for other designers to participate under the Barneys Green label.

I feel very positive about this growing environmental/creative/cultural movement. It signifies a major shift in the fashion consciousness. The time is right and the time is now. We all must work together to do our part to fuel the movement. We must educate ourselves and inform people on how to participate. Everything we do now must have a conscious thought to it. A more conscious process is possible. The future is thinking, talking and walking with the flag of intention to create beauty through fashion in a more organic, sustainable way. Barneys New York is making its best effort to do that with taste, an appreciation for luxury and a little bit of humor.

⸺⟨∞⟩⸺

The Consumption Crisis

Deborah J. C. Brosdahl, Associate Professor
Department of Apparel, Textiles and Interior
Design

College of Human Ecology
Kansas State University
Manhattan, KS

Kansas State University
199 Justin Hall
Manhattan, KS 66506

Sustainability requires a long-term outlook that encourages responsible consumption. Fashion, it seems, is fundamentally at odds with this goal. Perhaps apparel can be made sustainably, but fashion? Fashion is more than a product; fashion is a mode of thought. It affects everything from design to purchasing to obsolescence, and is usually distinguished by a fast-paced and ever-replenishing chain of supply and demand. The inevitable consequence of quick and constant change is ravenous resource consumption and a vast accumulation of waste. Better production methods can slow resource use and recycling can reduce waste, but buying (and therefore making) fewer products will address both problems.

Stemming consumption in America will be hard. The United States represents only five percent of the world's population, while its consumers use up approximately 25 percent of the world's natural resources. Our motivations for buying (sometimes more than we can afford or need) are complex and deeply rooted in our culture. Whether it's ordering a supersized McDonald's fries or purchasing yet another pair of Manolo Blahniks to add to the 100 pairs of shoes already in a closet bursting at the seams, clearly, sheer quantity is seductive. In addition, a basic human need is looking as though you belong to a place, a culture, a moment in time. It seems that Americans not only need to belong, we need to be better. We demonstrate our superiority through conspicuous consumption, and fashion lets us wear our aspirations on our sleeves.

Apparel long since ceased to simply protect us from the elements, and as soon as it did, it took on connotations of fashion. Probably since the last Ice Age, anything worn has communicated the wearer's sense of self and position in society. This is true whether the clothes in question are full-on Goth, a Diane von Furstenberg wrap dress and kitten heels, or a blue suit, white shirt and red tie. Specifically "fashionable" clothes (i.e., clothing promoted by the fashion industry) can enhance the consumer's status by communicating a person's ability to purchase products without regard to price (higher prices for new products are not necessarily related to higher quality), and a person's knowledge of what is "in." For many fashion leaders, fashion is addictive because it advertises how "with it" someone is with the newest and most cutting-edge ensembles.

Americans buy and buy and buy clothes. As a comparison between American and European spending habits demonstrates, our appetite for fashion is not simply an inevitable consequence of affluence and available choice. Let's look at Americans first. The most recent Bureau of Labor figures on consumer spending habits show that the average American family of three has approximately $44,400 (after taxes) to spend on everything it needs to sustain living. Of this, it spends approximately 11 percent on apparel and apparel services (laundry, dry cleaning, etc.). This works out to approximately $4,884 or $1,628 per person in a family per year—an increase over apparel spending for the several previous years. Now, let's look at the Europeans. On average, Europeans (of the 12 EU countries tallied) spend only seven percent of their disposable income on apparel and apparel services (according to www.eustatistics.gov.uk). Not only do Europeans spend less of their income on clothing, they: 1) don't focus on price as the first feature they look for when buying, 2) are willing to pay more for their clothing because they fully expect their clothes to be worn longer than do Americans, and 3) demand high-quality products. Could

Americans become more like Europeans in our apparel-buying habits? Should we?

Given the statistics related to ravenous apparel consumption and its attendant waste, I'm going to answer the second question with a "yes." For the sake of the environment (as well as their individual credit ratings!), Americans should buy fewer clothes. (They should buy less stuff, period, but that is beyond the scope of this article.) The answer to the first question is more elusive. I believe we can become more like Europeans in our buying habits, but realizing that possibility is complicated.

In the old adage "quality vs. quantity," quality is contrasted with quantity as if it's only possible to have one of these characteristics. Yet quality-loving Europeans do indeed buy less per year, and they still end up with closets full of clothing. This is possible because their higher quality-based purchases last longer than clothing designed solely with low price in mind.

However, the word "quality" invites interpretation. Indeed, noted quality assurance author, educator and researcher, Dr. Sara Kadolph of Iowa State University has concluded that when a person describes a product as "quality," she could be ascribing to it any number of positive attributes, among them: performance, features, reliability, conformance between design and function, durability, serviceability, aesthetics and other perceived quality issues, such as those related to brand name. Given the abundance of types of quality, do Americans value the right kind of quality, the kind of quality that would persuade them to be happy with less?

Before we can evaluate that question, we should first be explicit about what the right kind of quality would be. With an eye to reducing resource use and landfill, I propose that reliability (both in wear and care) and durability are necessary for a piece of apparel to escape being replaced after a season. In other words, the knit pullover can't sag and pill, the white shirt can't turn dingy grey and the coat placket can't have buttons hanging by a mere thread. Of course, sustainable fashion (not just apparel) is our challenge; I would be cheating if I didn't acknowledge that the piece has to stay genuinely fashionable, or at least attractive and wearable, for several seasons. I don't see this as an impossibility. While fashions come and go, surely we all have a few items that we have kept for years. The goal would be to keep most of our items for many years and only acquire very few new pieces a year.

So, do Americans appreciate this kind of quality? There's some evidence that they do. Relatively recently, my research revealed that even teenagers respect quality. After conducting several studies related to apparel shopping behavior in 12- to 18-year-olds, it came to light that the kids interviewed were aware that quality is supposed to be an important consideration when shopping for clothing. When pressed for an answer about what quality meant to them, the children said that the clothes they bought should be long-lasting. They were probably repeating what they'd heard from their parents.

While it's nice to know that a reverence for quality is still being passed down from generation to generation in America, actions speak louder than words. Widespread American devotion to stores like Old Navy and H&M suggests that our working definition of quality has more to do with achieving the highest quantity to dollar ratio. According to this understanding, the consumer "wins" by being able to acquire a lot with practically no money, leaving her with a lot of money left over, which represents a lot of new opportunities to buy more. Obviously, this kind of quality holds no promise for curing shopaholism and overconsumption, and results in a cycle of demanding more and more for less and less. This buying philosophy is not good for society, consumers or the apparel industry.

The European meaning of quality conjures an image of the artisan hunched over his bench, painstakingly stitching away. Europeans tend to assess quality by how an object measures up to the ideal (defined in part by traditions of craftsmanship). The European consumer "wins" by buying the most "perfect" object. Having achieved her aim, she takes pride in the object for its own sake, an attitude which reduces the chance that she will want to replace it quickly. Quality à la Europe seems like a concept that can quell consumption.

Although Americans give a lot of lip service (and mostly just lip service) to quality in their apparel, the mere fact that the adolescents did identify quality as a good thing suggests to me that quality is not so foreign to Americans that we cannot learn to appreciate it fully. Like taste, an eye for quality can be developed.

Ideally, industry professionals would educate consumers about quality. They are in a prime position to do so. Wouldn't it be great if retail brands used their marketing materials to convince customers that improved quality (and increased price) is, in fact, a good thing, because in the long run they will pay less per wear with a longer-lasting item? Or what if industry leaders let consumers know that by paying more for something they'll never want to throw away, they will not only have something they'll love, but they will also be contributing to a cleaner planet?

Would such ground-breaking tactics cause companies to lose sales and, therefore, income? Not necessarily. A calculated price increase could offset lower sales volume. Better yet, if companies demonstrate how higher prices fund higher wages, more U.S. jobs and responsible environmental stewardship, that could create a devoted customer base. If the same amount of money currently spent on advertising low prices were spent instead on advertising the advantages of purchasing longer-lasting and higher-quality apparel, perhaps consumers would change their purchasing habits.

Reality check: Very, very few brands even try to make these claims. Retailers rarely focus on the quality characteristics mentioned previously, especially features such as reliability and durability. As the monumental success of Wal-Mart demonstrates, cheap makes money! For at least several decades, purchases have increasingly been driven by lower prices. And inexpensive mass production makes money because consumers support it. Well, no wonder. In a marketplace characterized by indifferent quality and buy-one-get-one-free retail gimmicks, who can blame Americans for basing their purchasing decisions on the lowest price? The unfortunate upshot of this is that Americans have been desensitized to quality. (Possibly most of us couldn't even recognize its hallmarks if we tried). Ironically, the race for low prices has also resulted in companies' losing profitability and being forced to move overseas, where they can produce more cheaply and thus give consumers the price they demand—for now. It seems inevitable that, unless we completely ignore worker equity, the price of goods must bottom out. When it does, companies will look for a way to differentiate themselves and justify raising their prices. A return to quality is one way they might do that.

I hope consumers will call for industry change before that. As Thomas Friedman pointed out in his bestseller, The World is Flat, every buying decision a consumer makes is a vote indicating their support or lack of support for how companies conduct business. Consumer power was decisively proven in the apparel industry during the great "midi" disaster of the 1970s. After several seasons of selling miniskirts, the fashion industry deemed it time for the "mini" to cycle into obsolescence and attempted to introduce a new, longer style called the "midiskirt." In a proud statement of rebellion, women refused to give up their short skirts to embrace the new style. Firms in the fashion industry were left with millions of unsold midis, as well as the realization that consumer demand was the true industry driver.

But who else can get consumers excited about quality? The answer is simple: Teachers. Being a professor myself, I strongly believe in the power of curriculum to catalyze societal change. Teachers can impart skills and concepts that will help students identify quality in apparel, and understand the effect of their buying habits on their own lifestyle as well as on the environment and on other human beings. In part, I blame a lack of educational resources for the ongoing surge in overconsumption, and the average person's general ignorance about how products are made. In recent years, the programs that have traditionally exposed kids to important issues related to clothing purchasing have been wiped out by slashed budgets for public education and the Department of Agriculture.

Home economics programs (now known under various pseudonyms such as Human Environmental Sciences, etc.) and 4-H programs had their heyday in the 1950s, through the 1970s. Started in the 1800s as a way for young women to be self-sufficient (by sewing their own clothes, for instance), home economics evolved in the latter 1900s as a program to shape young men and women into resourceful and knowledgeable consumers. Similarly, one goal of today's 4-H programs is to teach kids not only how to make clothing, but also how to manage an apparel budget and to determine if apparel is well made. It is within the scope of such programs to include information on how clothing is manufactured, and to emphasize the consumer's responsibility to seek out companies that pay their employees living wages and use organic fibers or nontoxic dyes. As home economics and 4-H programs have declined in number and importance, issues such as sustainability have become more problematic and widespread. I don't think that this is a coincidence.

Can apparel and fashion be sustainable? The answer is yes, but only if Americans change their way of thinking. To do this, apparel industry leaders, home economics teachers and 4-H leaders (to name just a few) can join forces and help convince the next generation of consumers that buying better and fewer clothes will not only benefit them, but also the planet.

Tomorrow Is the New Now

Horst Rechelbacher, Founder
Intelligent Nutrients, Aveda

Intelligent Nutrients
983 East Hennepin Avenue
Minneapolis, MN 55414
(612) 617-2000
Press Contact:
(914) 381-1843

Fashion, by definition, is about the now. It's about newness, and the excitement this newness creates. So it strikes me as paradoxical that the majority of today's fashion design is, by and large, relying on old, detrimental ways of thinking. It gives very poignant meaning to the phrase "fashion victim." Though there are earth-conscious designers at work, if the rest of us don't evolve our concept of fashion, we're in big trouble.

This horrifying state of affairs is what led me to reach my long-term goal of designing beauty products that are 100 percent food grade organic for my new company, Intelligent Nutrients. After nearly 40 years in the beauty business, I have learned a lot about what it means to be sustainable. Because the cosmetic companies are not beholden to the standards of food grade rating systems, they can call themselves organic if some of their ingredients are organic—yet the rest of the composition could be, and oftentimes is, dangerously toxic.

That's why it's so important to consult the organic movement or, even better, become a part of it. For instance, for a food product to claim that it's organic, it must be made with 70 percent organic ingredients, certified to U.S. standards, and the remaining 30 percent must be made up of agricultural, non-toxic substances. For 100 percent certified food grade organic status, all ingredients must be certified to U.S. standards. Alternately, for simple "organic" status, 95 percent of ingredients must be certified organic to U.S. standards, and the remaining five percent must be food grade, non-toxic agricultural substances approved for inclusion in organic products by the USDA. If beauty products were food grade organic, they would be subject to USDA approval. Most of them would be off the shelves in a heartbeat, which is where they belong if the world is to maintain a healthy pulse.

Truly captivating fashion is design that improves the world we live in. There's a weighty amount of scientific evidence that tells us we cannot continue to pollute our planet the way we've been doing for the last couple of centuries. It's critical that consumers have easy, simple guidance for choosing safely. The best example comes from the organic movement. All materials—from fabrics to the raw ingredients in cosmetics—need to be sourced from organically grown food substances. Does this seem extreme? I don't think so. In fact, I find it to be our sole, sane option.

- *It protects the elements*
  Eliminating pesticides, synthetic fertilizers and genetically modified organisms (GMOs) keeps the soil, waterways and the atmosphere healthy.

- *It protects us*
  Because we drink water, breathe air, eat food, clothe and cleanse our body, there's no way to insulate ourselves from the toxins in the elements.

- *It's easily recognizable*
  Certified organic food is a quick, recognizable assurance to consumers that what they put on and in their bodies is non-toxic.

- *It helps slow climate change*
  Organically farmed soil is higher in rich carbon-based matter. More carbon is held in the soil that would otherwise be released into the air. This helps curb our already excessive carbon footprint, which is leading to global warming.

- *It's authentic*
  True fashion is about non-toxicity. If fashion pollutes, it should no longer be called fashion, it should be called pollution.

- *It just makes sense*

  It's wise to only put on your body something that wouldn't harm you if you swallowed it.

So where do we begin? Again, we look to organics. Let's take cotton as an easy target. It's not only one of the world's most chemically-dependent crops, but in the U.S., 70 percent of cotton production also relies on genetically-modified seeds. A single t-shirt uses about nine ounces of cotton, an average of 17 tea-spoons of synthetic fertilizers and nearly a teaspoon of pesticides that are classified as among the most toxic by the U.S. Environmental Protection Agency. It's easy to make the short leap in logic: conventional cotton farming is dangerous to our air, earth and water, and it's been scientifically linked to cancer.

Fibers, especially micro-fibers, which are synthetic and petroleum-derived, are perilous to our lungs. Tiny dust particles—micro-dust—coat our lungs, potentially inducing lung cancer. Fabric dyes can also be quite dangerous. Some even use cadmium, which, with exposure to the air, binds to small particles. It falls to the ground or water as rain or snow, and may contaminate fish, plants, and animals.

If there's any positive fallout from global climate change, it's this: We know there's no separation of humans from their environment. What harms the planet also harms us. Any farming or manufacturing that does not follow the intrinsic order of the natural world ultimately destroys it. Ecosystems are disrupted from over-harvesting, from pesticide use, from logging, from water contamination, and from greenhouse gas emissions. And when we consider the consequences of GMOs, our situation becomes drastically more dangerous. Fifty percent of the U.S. bee population has died in the last three months. Scientists suspect this is linked to GMO farming. Plant and insect species are on the front lines. They are the first to be endangered, and their absence wreaks havoc on our living systems. Yet our environment is the foundation of all living systems.

Fashion and beauty, design and manufacturing are harming the Earth, but they can also help to restore it. In fact, if we look to the origins of fashion, we trace it to where it's still thriving without harming the environment or humankind. I've learned much of what it means to be sustainable from indigenous people. These groups live all over the world and yet their designs are similar in practice and meaning. They serve not only to attract and adorn, but to protect, nourish and repel. Their face paints, to take one example, function as sunscreen, nutrition for the body, and insect repellent. Their cosmetics are not only safe, but are vibrant, nourishing and conditioning to the skin, providing hydration and protection from sun and mosquitoes.

Compare that to our beauty products. Recently I received an email from a friend asking me to forward it to all the women I knew. It named several major cosmetics companies that use lead in their lipsticks.

Lead is about as dangerous as it gets, and we are putting it on our mouths! The Campaign for Safe Cosmetics (CSC) is doing a tremendous job trying to educate the public about the dangerous ingredients in many major brands. According to the CSC, major loopholes in federal law allow the $35 billion cosmetics industry to put unlimited amounts of chemicals into personal care products with no required testing, no monitoring of health effects, and inadequate labeling requirements. The European Union bans 1,100 ingredients, but the U.S. prohibits only nine.

It's crucial to understand regulations so that we're not fooled by the "greenwashing" of design. Whether it's clothing, cosmetics, fragrances, cleansers, homes, offices or even furniture design, good design is non-toxic. No exceptions.

We've been warned by the United Nations that we have a ten-year window to reverse the damage we have done. We can look upon this news as dreadful—or, as creatives, we can revel in the opportunity to reinvent. And the world is ready. The savvy consumer wants good, healthy design. Design that isn't just "eco," but is also "chic." Just as the days are numbered for products that pollute, the days of the same old "eco" look are up. No one wants boring. What a wonderful time to be a designer! As with all artistic disciplines, self-imposed limits can create original solutions.

I believe it's within our reach. Remember, at one time we were all organic. Today, it takes imagination to return to thinking the way the world's shamans thought—to use completely holistic thought processes to create beauty and sophisticated style in a way that supports all the senses, and the sense of well being for our planet and ourselves; to use modern technology like nano- and microtechnology to test the safety of our products; to help us decide if we are on the right path with our designs, and if we're not on the correct path, to keep looking for it! But all these steps must be accompanied by the deep under-standing that the planet does not belong to us—it is we who belong to it. And ultimately, it's merely on loan from future generations.

SECTION 2:

MAPPING THE FUTURE OF FABRICS

Deconstructing "The Perfect T-Shirt"

Mike Betts, Director
better thinking ltd.

Unit 23
Links Yard
Spelman Street
London E1 5LX
www.betterthinking.co.uk

Whahat does the phrase "the perfect t-shirt" mean to you? A perfectly fitted t-shirt? A shirt that is amazingly high quality? A sustainable t-shirt? Through a public, hands-on study of conscientious and viable garment production, we at better thinking have challenged ourselves to create a t-shirt that is all of these things and more—quite a daunting task, given that none of us had any experience in apparel or textiles before we began.

Better thinking is an ethical branding consultancy that creates dramatic and effective ways for businesses to become more inspirational and successful. We have chosen the humble t-shirt as the vehicle for our endeavor, based on the logic that almost everybody on the planet owns one and will therefore have a vested interest in the environmental and social impact of its production. Even though we are not about to go into t-shirt-making, our findings from "the perfect t-shirt" project can be applied far beyond the textile industry, giving us a better understanding of the challenges facing any business attempting to green up its act. Moreover, we hope our project will inform the public of the current barriers to sustainable production, as well as increase visibility and support for ventures that are developing successful green solutions.

In our team's effort to take into account every possible aspect of t-shirt manufacture, we consider how to obtain the raw material (e.g. cultivation practices and resource use), turn it into a t-shirt (shipping, factory power, working conditions and dyes), understand the issues involved in use (laundering, quality and longevity), and discover what happens to it at the end of its life (recycling, composting or landfilling). This is the stripped-down version. Our blog lists 60 different questions identifying the things we'd like to know about our shirt.

We realized early on that tradeoffs would be inevitable. We quickly found ourselves embroiled in earnest debates, such as: Is sending the raw material 5,000 miles away to a ground-breaking green factory worth it? What about using more chemicals to make a t-shirt that uses less water by staying fresh longer? Or producing a shirt in natural tones rather than bright white, even if this decision may make it less popular and therefore less world-changing?

Ultimately, there are no best answers. The textile industry is still in the first stages of turning itself around, and every environmentally positive decision puts strain on other links in the chain. The good news is that if the infrastructure existed, there could in fact be many different types of "the perfect t-shirt." They could be made in different locations from different materials by different methods. But for the time being, we have to accept that there are gaps in each chain that necessitate compromise.

Accepting that our t-shirt exists in the real world— and not every material, tool, energy source, transport method and person involved in its production can leave no environmental footprint—we've decided to implement a deeply conscious approach, justifying every decision we make. An alternative title for the project could have been, "The World's Most Considered T-shirt."

To demonstrate our commitment to finding a truly progressive solution, we invited constructive criticism on our blog by posting everything we've learned (except for a few key facts which could make us vulnerable to copycats). Through debating, voting and requesting feedback on the Web site, we sought the public's active involvement.

This approach to dialogue and interaction helps everyone untangle the issues surrounding the global, $400 billion garment industry.

Before getting started, we could have confidently described what we thought the final product would look like: affordable, soft, knitted, pure white, 100 percent cotton. In short, it would be identical to a well-made designer shirt, with the only difference being the extra-special feeling of buying a t-shirt made with the utmost environmental and social consideration. Now, 12 months wiser, we have come to realize that, at present, it isn't possible to mass-produce a hardcore ethical t-shirt that looks like a conventional shirt. For example, the existing infrastructure for a natural dye process (which is only more environmentally sound in some respects) can produce runs of 20,000 shirts, maximum. Knowing that companies like Nike, the Gap or H&M consider a run of 100,000 shirts to be on the small side, you can understand why it's not viable for them to pursue such an option. This led us to change an initial description of the project. At the outset called it "a blueprint for an industry." That eventually became something more appropriate: "Inspiration for an industry, progress through transparent communication."

First, we tried to find an appropriate green factory situated close to where the raw material was obtained, thereby avoiding the several tons of emissions created by long-distance transportation.

Ethical manufacturers proved scarce and presented us with some considerable downsides. In one instance, a manufacturer prototyped a hand-woven shirt that was rougher and less pleasant to wear than a conventional, machine-knitted t-shirt. Its aesthetic and its greener, socially-constructive manufacturing process did present advantages, but the scratchiness and lack of elasticity would have made it less popular, reducing the positive impacts of the project as a whole.

When we finally found a factory producing machine-knitted shirts using green energy, the supplier was based on another continent. We decided it was worth the shipping fuel to promote such forward-thinking methods of production. But then we received their samples. Some of the shirts were stitched crookedly; hems were uneven when clearly they shouldn't have been, neck and shoulder seams didn't line up, and joints were bunched up together too tightly. While this wasn't the case with every shirt, it seemed incredibly wasteful to grow the raw material, transport it to the factory, weave it, dye it, and then stitch some of the shirts so badly they couldn't be sold. At the time of writing, we have yet to choose our manufacturer.

Bleaching presented a second major challenge. Typically, t-shirt fibers are bleached in a treatment bath, which is then discharged into wastewater streams, disrupting ecosystems and threatening aquatic life. We discovered that while it is technically

possible to bleach a shirt in a completely environmentally sound way, this requires an innovative
closed loop system (i.e., the treatment bath is completely reused). We are struggling to find suppliers
who really consider the environment in their manufacturing processes, let alone ones who are so
committed they have actually invested in the most
advanced technologies available.

Dyeing and transportation were easier to figure out.
The conventional dye process discharges massive
quantities of toxic chemicals into the environment,
including huge amounts of dioxins, the world's
number one carcinogen. Of 1,600 dye chemicals
available, only 16 are approved by the EPEA as
sound for our health and the environment. Our
eventual solution to the color problem (an issue for
which we have written a detailed report, available
on the project Web site) was to avoid color completely. Leaving the shirt undyed eliminates a very
toxic part of the production process.

Shipping can represent a significant factor in carbon footprint calculations, yet it is often ignored.
We pledged to pursue transportation routes that
balance commercial efficiency with environmental
concerns, and to encourage renewable technologies
wherever possible within the supply chain.

As you can see, assembling our supply chain is a
complex, difficult challenge. We hope our trials
and successes will indicate what can and should be

expected of the textile industry now, as well as where it can make future improvements. Quite frankly, we found almost all government bodies and NGOs to be less than helpful as sources of information or support. (Not through any unwillingness to help on their part, but purely because much information about sustainability does not exist in ways that are commercially helpful.) This in part explains why the textile industry has done so little up to this point to push the boundaries. Even though we are newcomers in the textile industry, one government source told us we were "at the cutting edge of sustainable textiles." Not good!

Similarly, we've encountered other people within the industry reluctant to share their own knowledge. Understandably, they've spent time and money finding out what they know, and on a few occasions we've had to employ similar tactics to protect our own competitive advantage. However, we share whenever we can, as a purely commercial approach hinders the greater good by making it incredibly difficult for manufacturers to adopt the technological improvements necessary for greener manufacturing.

More openly sharing knowledge might make it easier on the supplier's end, the most static part of the chain. Suppliers have good reason to move slowly. Of everyone in the system, they have the most invested in the current, unsustainable infrastructure. Therefore, they run the greatest risk trying to change it. Switching to cutting-edge green machinery, re-training staff, and disposing of waste properly requires a significant initial outlay. However, suppliers that prioritize green methods now will be winners in the long run. Green suppliers are so rare that improvements as simple as switching to a renewable power source—often involving no more than a phone call—can result in a significant competitive advantage. This is in addition to the environmental benefit of reducing fossil fuel use.

After viewing the situation from the textile industry's perspective, we have gained some sympathy. Yet we are also somewhat shocked by how little the industry has tried to push the boundaries. While significant barriers to the mass production of ethical t-shirts remain, it is entirely reasonable to demand that all manufacturers commit to some form of continuous improvement. A business could introduce a small percentage of organic fiber, or plan to eliminate all synthetic chemicals used in its factories by the end of a particular year, or launch a range of clothing produced using solar power. The initiatives don't need to be groundbreaking! The commitment behind them just needs to move us all forward—encouraging suppliers to offer larger-scale, greener manufacturing methods, gradually raising industry standards, making customers more aware of ethical issues, and pushing governments to introduce more advanced legislation.

There seems to be a very healthy concern among companies that consumers will disregard their environmental improvements. They fear that consumers, out of cynicism or ignorance, won't take into account the constraints of a complicated supply chain that only allows for gradual reform. As a result, some companies imagine their well-meant efforts backfiring, damaging the brand. In response to this concern, we urge companies to increase transparency. By letting customers know what they are doing and why (as well as what they're not doing and why), and how they intend to improve, businesses can win support for their attempts to introduce ethical improvements.

Realizing that things have to change is a start. If no one knows about the problem, there is no motivation to try to fix it. After that, there's a need for concrete information: the kind that shows people tangible ways they can take action and make choices as businesspeople, as shoppers and as human beings. Ultimately, we need to remember that the support and encouragement of others is just as important as what we do ourselves

Eco-Fabrics: Balancing Fashion and Ideals

Susan and Yves Gagnon, Owners
SYKA™ Textiles Trading Corp.

32933 Boothby Ave.
Mission, BC
V2V 7R3
www.syka.ca

The demand for eco-friendly fashions has sky-rocketed. When we founded SYKA™ Textiles, most North American designers were skeptical that the concepts "fashionable" and "eco-friendly" could coexist. "Perish the idea! We're not making dungarees. We're in the business of fashion!" But with initiatives like FutureFashion, leaders in the field incorporated new fabrics into their designs, educated their customers, and created new niche markets. The excitement of eco-fashion had begun.

As textile wholesalers, we were thrilled to see beautiful fabrics whose production had less of a negative environmental impact. Our goal was very clear: to make stunning, high-quality, eco-friendly fabrics accessible to the fashion industry. We did this by launching the first-ever brand of eco-friendly fabrics, the Eco-Lux™ Collection. However, since SYKA™'s inception, one of the greatest challenges we have faced is striking a balance between the ideals that define and shape what makes a fabric eco-friendly and meeting the particular demands of the fashion market. This has been exciting as well as frustrating, since both forces are dynamic and, when considered together, often appear at odds.

We find that the expansion and success of eco-friendly fabrics in fashion depend strongly on compatibility between the green movement, market demand, and the strong business skills required in this industry.

As a result of the explosion in environmental concern, businesses seeking to become "greener" face many options. Unfortunately, the trend has also brought with it many unsubstantiated claims from advertisements, magazines, and of course, the Internet. Rather than using solid scientific evidence, these claims often take a very emotional and moralistic more-perfect-and-pure-than-thou position. Often misusing all of the latest buzzwords, they compare the "greenness" of various eco-fibers and fabrics (complete with winners) and make lists of too-good-to-be-true fabric properties that are not substantiated. We acknowledge our bias. At the same time we firmly believe that if businesses circulate unproven information, green improvements are less likely to occur. Eco-fashion simply becomes a short-term way to capitalize on a passing trend, and may end up doing more damage than good.

We feel it's necessary to clarify, as best we can, some of the "green" qualifiers used in the fashion industry and how they relate to fabric and fashion.

In fashion fabrics, much confusion arises from the misuse of the terms "natural," "organic," and "eco-friendly." These terms have often been used inter-changeably, diluting any specific meaning. For instance, "natural" and "organic" are not the same. Yet we have many people asking us for "natural" or "organic" fabrics, while actually meaning "eco-friendly." "Natural" means that the fiber has been harvested and produced with minimal human pro-cessing. For today's most popular fibers, this usually means cotton, wool, silk and linen. In apparel, unless specified (and certified) otherwise, natural fibers are not organic. To qualify a fiber as "organic," as in "organic cotton," fiber production must adhere to strict standards and be certified by the appropriate governing body. The Organic Trade Association has clear and comprehensive information on this matter. For producers who go to great lengths to make a cer-tified organic product, it must be extremely frustrat-ing to see conventional fibers marketed as "organic."

An "eco-friendly" fiber may or may not be natural and/or organic. What it unequivocally does not mean is that the fiber has zero negative environmental impact. We do not know of any fiber that has zero negative impact. Certainly, all production has some.

The most straightforward way to define an "eco-friendly" fiber is by specifying that at least one major step in its production has less of a negative environmental impact than the conventional alternative. For example, bamboo, soy, and hemp fibers are eco-friendly because their production requires lower levels of herbicide and pesticide usage compared to conventional cotton. Similarly, organic cotton, a natural, certified organic fiber, is also eco-friendly for this reason. All of these fibers bio-degrade at a faster rate than petroleum-based fibers such as polyester and nylon, and come from resources that may be renewed. These fibers, as well as others, make up a large portion of the new "green" fibers used for fashion, and their usage is an important step in the right direction.

FROM ECO-FIBERS TO ECO-FABRICS

Ultimately, it is the fabrics that are important in fashion. If eco-fibers are gentler on the environment than the conventional alternative, we must identify which stage(s) of fabric production has a less negative environmental impact. There are numerous stages in fabric production, and if all are not considered, it is next to impossible to discern the relative "eco-friendliness" of one fabric over another. With the widening concern over the environmental impact of the fashion industry, there are many opinions on which fabrics are better. We don't see how these conclusions can be drawn, because there have been no good comparisons of the overall process. At this point, we can only compare, at best, one stage in the process and ask ourselves, "How does this fabric's stage of production compare with another fabric, in terms of negative environmental impact?"

The first stage of production relates to fiber production, and is the main focus considered for most eco-friendly fabrics like bamboo, soy, hemp and lyocell (commonly known as Tencel®). Matters such as irrigation levels, natural or chemical fertilizer use, herbicide and pesticide use, land availability, speed at which source plants grow and replenish, and the overall treatment of animals needed to produce hair or silk all must be considered.

After the fiber production, the second major stage is yarn spinning. Issues here include the energy and materials used to process the fibers, the type of dyestuff used (e.g., for yarn-dyed fabrics), as well as the actual waste by-product derived from the different processes. Lyocell is environmentally friendly because the solution used in the yarn fabrication is not flushed into the environment.

The third stage is the actual fabric production. This differs according to the particular standards of each weaving and knitting mill, and/or dye house. Mills and dye houses concerned with producing eco-friendly fabrics will often obtain international certifications for compliance (see below). In addition to considerations of energy use and other by-products when making greige fabrics, energy and water usage along with dyeing/finishing multi-phase processes are extremely important factors. If the fabric is to be used to make fashionable garments, then it needs to be dyed and finished to certain specifications. Here, the important steps in the process become the type of dyestuff used, the application of toxic mordants to improve fastness, the other chemicals and solvents used in the finishing process, the energy and water required for dyeing and finishing the fabric, and the extent of runoff and wastewater treatment. Reactive dyes, commonly known as "low impact dyes," vary in terms of environmental friendliness depending on the type used and the manufacturer. In general, however, they are gentler on the environment than conventional dyes, because they are more efficiently absorbed resulting in less polluting runoff. These dyes are used in Eco-Lux™ fabrics.

Finally, for the last step of post-production, the distance and transportation required to ship the fabric to the garment manufacturing plant and eventually, to the end consumer are factors to consider when determining if a product is eco-friendly.

These steps offer a very rough framework in the production process, but illustrate the numerous points at which the environment can be affected by fabric manufacturing. This obviously does not begin to address the very important and related subject of fair and ethical conditions for workers. We are not aware of any published scientific study by an unbiased third party that has come close to addressing these numerous steps in fabric production. This would be a monumental task, but one that we feel the scientific community should address.

ECO-FABRICS IN THE FASHION MARKET

Author Katherine Govier said, "When everything is fashion, the only genius is timing," and all indicators tell us that the time is ripe for eco-fashion. Al Gore's documentary "An Inconvenient Truth," and British entrepreneur Sir Richard Branson's financial commitment to combat the threat of climate change have helped bring green concerns to the forefront of the public agenda. In Vancouver, Canada, where SYKA™ was founded, preferential consideration is given to green businesses competing for contracts for the upcoming 2010 Winter Olympics. In fashion, we have seen companies such as Patagonia and, more recently, the U.K.-based retailers Marks & Spencer and Tesco successfully make headway in this arena. Will this trend to be replaced as quickly as it arrived, or will it endure?

The term "sustainable" is not one we use often, because its meaning seems to have been lost. From our perspective, "sustainability" refers to long-term objectives that are both environmental and economical. The definition of sustainable development, as originally drafted by the World Commission on Environment and Development in 1987, refers to "meeting the needs of the present generation without compromising the needs of future generations." As such, development policies and environmental protection are not at odds, as both aim to increase people's overall welfare. In fashion, this means that environmental and business practices need to interact often to keep up with a fast-paced and changing industry. Using the environment as a canvas for strategy, businesses must be able to provide the right product at the right time, and at the right price.

Supplying the right fabrics for fashion has both intuitive as well as pragmatic elements. Fashion is a product of many factors including culture, geography, and cycles that turn at an ever-increasing speed. Even though fashion is currently considering green issues, television shows like "Ugly Betty," and movies like "The Devil Wears Prada," remind us that the industry is generally portrayed with a certain lightness in relation to serious world issues. In order to be used more extensively in fashion, eco-fabrics must complement fashion design with high quality.

The intuitive element in our work is finding the right quality, texture, hand, style, weight and color of fabric. Almost all eco-friendly fabrics have wonderful tactile properties, but we have found that the job of successfully sourcing consistently high-quality and fashionable fabrics requires a substantial investment of time and resources. We travel around the world and attend major textile trade fairs to learn what's up and coming. We also consult fashion experts, monitor industry publications and, of course, listen to our customers' input.

Finding and achieving what is fashionable is no small feat, especially when working with some of the new eco-fibers. Bamboo and soy, while wonderfully soft, are new and the quality can be highly variable. Hasty production, lack of experience with new fibers and less-than-optimal technology can add up to frequent defects. Because we have built a reputation around quality with Eco-Lux™, we take a number of steps to ensure a solid, environmentally sound product rather than a quick fabric fix for a booming market.

When we source our fabrics, we also source our suppliers. Of the numerous mills we visit annually, we shortlist the ones that not only have the technology to produce beautiful fabric with minimal defects, but also stand behind their words with good business practices. We test and monitor our fabrics and develop strong relationships with our mills. We visit the mills in person several times a year. We also seek international certification and verification from mills, such as ISO 9001, ISO 14001 and Oeko-Tex Standard 100. We have developed relationships with serious mills that care about quality and eco-friendly fabrics. This approach also helps us to customize and develop new and unique fabrics.

The issue of price is a contentious one when it comes to eco-friendly fabrics. If the industry is to become more environmentally friendly, eco-fabrics should be reasonably accessible and affordable. However, as it currently stands, if variables such as quality and quantity are controlled, eco-friendly fibers or fabrics cost more. This is because there is less supply, fewer suppliers, and quickly increasing demand. While it's likely that prices will fall as supply increases, it's doubtful that these fibers will ever cost as little as conventional ones.

Recent media reports have suggested that sustainable fashion can be had for the same cost as conventional clothing. This builds unrealistic expectations for consumers, which leads to disappointment when faced with a higher price tag. When uniqueness (as in eco-friendly fibers) and quality are demanded along with low prices, there's always something in the equation, such as fair trade, that has to give. Implementing environmentally friendly practices comes at an added cost. If there was none, the debate would be needless, because changing our ways would be cheaper and thus swift and easy. Ultimately, the consumer must be willing to pay extra for an eco-friendly garment, at least until regulation forces all producers to meet these standards.

If we are to improve the health of our planet and build a sustainable future, the massive international garment industry must adopt the eco-friendly movement. We have seen amazing strides in the improvement of the quality, availability and impact of eco-fabrics, but there is still plenty of work to be done. Green businesses must start to acknowledge that eco-friendly fabrics are worth pursuing and not a fading trend. There is no quick solution. In fabric and fashion, we have the choice to turn around some of the environmental consequences of rapid industrialization.

Hemp Goes Straight

Lawrence Serbin, President & Owner
Hemp Traders

2132 Colby Ave. Suite #5
Los Angeles, CA 90025
www.hemptraders.com

When I first decided to start a business that emphasized environmental concerns, I thought of hemp, the one-time major American farm crop for which our colonial forefathers had found hundreds of uses: rope, paper, textiles and sails. Wanting to deepen my understanding of hemp's potential, I put on my best suit and tie, shined my shoes, grabbed a briefcase and headed for a meeting of a brand new organization, The Business Alliance for Commerce in Hemp (BACH). I was prepared for a power meeting on rebuilding a viable hemp industry. Instead, I entered a cloudy room full of hippies smoking pot.

Hemp has not generally benefited from its association with marijuana. Since 1938, its cultivation in America has been outlawed due to hysteria over its botanical cousin. People commonly confuse marijuana with hemp. Industrial hemp contains an insignificant amount of the psychoactive cannabinoid, THC. The amount is so low that it is impossible to get high from smoking or ingesting it. Moreover, hemp contains a relatively high percentage of another cannabinoid, CBD, that actually blocks the effects of THC. Hemp, it turns out, is not only not marijuana; it could be called "antimarijuana."

In addition, the popularity of hemp textiles has been compromised by (again) association with the kind of alternative lifestyle that tolerates a certain lack of sartorial refinement. It is too bad that hemp has been bogged down by cultural prejudice rather than considered on its own merits. (However, Giorgio Armani, a textile connoisseur and fashion icon who has become synonymous with sophistication, uses hemp in both denim and suits.) An important component of my role as the president of Hemp Traders is to educate both my buyers and the general public on the history and current uses of hemp, in order to dispel the common misconceptions.

Pot-smoking hippies didn't deter me from learning about hemp. Some of them helped. Many BACH members proved to be knowledgeable, excited, and committed. I befriended the group's founder, Chris Conrad, and eventually served as its national director for a year and a half. My research led me to the conclusion that selling hemp fabric would be a good business to develop. Hemp textiles sell at a price only slightly higher than cotton or linen, and they could be used for a very wide range of products and markets. At the end of 1993, my first shipment of hemp textiles arrived in the Port of Los Angeles.

I soon realized the difficulty of selling a new fabric to buyers who had never heard of hemp. Most of them were used to dealing with flax, and felt they had no reason to purchase this "new type of linen" whose only difference (in their eyes) was the higher price. Most of the regular buyers of fabric in the Los Angeles area told me that I was being foolish.

Fortunately, people's concerns about health and the environment are leading them to choose products that address those issues. A question I frequently hear in my profession is, "How does the use of hemp make a product greener or better?" There are several reasons.

From a sustainability viewpoint, hemp offers a clear advantage over other fabrics. As a vegetable (as opposed to a petroleum-based) fiber, hemp is biodegradable and a renewable resource. As hemp plants grow and build up cellulosic fiber, they remove five times the carbon dioxide from the atmosphere as the same acreage of trees. Hemp is also an extremely efficient crop. It produces more fiber yield per acre than any other source: one hemp harvest yields 250 percent more fiber than cotton and 600 percent more fiber than flax on the same amount of land. Moreover, hemp can be harvested about 120 days after seeding, up to three harvests per year.

One might think that such high production strains the land and water supply, but actually, hemp cultivation is easy on the earth. In stark contrast to cotton, hemp is a hardy plant that thrives without chemicals. Its broad leaves block the sunlight, preventing weeds from growing. Where the ground permits, hemp's strong roots—which can descend three feet—anchor the soil, protecting it from runoff. The topsoil and subsoil structures of a hemp field resemble those of forests. Hemp plants shed their leaves all through the growing season, adding nitrogen-rich organic matter to the topsoil and helping it retain moisture. Farmers have reported excellent growth on land that has been cultivated steadily for nearly 100 years.

Last but not least, hemp represents an excellent choice for sustainable textiles because almost all parts of the plant can be used in a variety of applications, from plastics to paper to food to biodiesel.

The benefits of hemp extend beyond cultivation practices. Hemp fiber facilitates energy and water conservation during textile processing. All hemps are bast fibers (including ramie and flax). They're cellulosic and are located just beneath the bark in the stalk, which makes them more durable than cotton fibers. Cotton is also cellulosic, but it's taken from the boll and therefore weaker). Hemp garments wear out slowly, requiring relatively few replacements and thus save money and energy. Hemp is also more porous than cotton, allowing fabrics made from it to breathe and to absorb water. Hemp fiber takes up and retains color well, minimizing dye waste. Hemp is naturally resistant to mold, bacteria and ultraviolet light.

In the past, an important technical barrier to widespread hemp use was the coarseness of the fiber. Traditional methods to soften vegetable fibers used acids to remove lignin, a type of natural glue found in many plant fibers. While this method worked well with cotton or flax, it weakened the hemp fibers, leaving them too unstable to use. Then in the mid-1980s, researchers developed an enzymatic process to successfully remove lignin from the hemp fiber without compromising its strength. For the first time in history, de-gummed hemp fiber could be spun alone or with other fibers (wool, cotton, lyocell and silk, just to name some possibilities) to produce fine textiles for apparel. This technological breakthrough has catapulted hemp to the forefront of modern textile design and fashion. I stock 100 percent fine hemp linen that weighs 4.6 ounces. I also carry hemp fleece and hemp/silk blends. Hemp/organic cotton t-shirts are environmentally responsible and take advantage of the softness of cotton and the superior breathability and anti-bacterial properties of hemp.

Currently, hemp textiles occupy a small but growing market. About 45 percent goes into apparel, another 45 percent goes into home furnishings, and ten percent into accessories or footwear. Demand has been growing due to the popularity of environmental products, the increase in quality and selection of hemp-based fibers as well as the lower cost.

Despite all hemp has to offer, there is about 100 times more cotton being grown throughout the world. This difference can partly be explained by the substantial subsidies that uphold the cotton economy, particularly here in the U.S. Pure hemp is about double the price of cotton and about one and a half times the cost of linen. Hemp/cotton blends are the same price as linen and about 50 percent higher than cotton.

The price of hemp will go down when more acreage is grown, its by-products are used for other purposes and hemp-processing technology is brought into the 21st century. Most textile hemp is manufactured in China, with a much smaller portion coming from Romania. In these developing countries, it's still economically viable to use human labor to soften the hemp and remove the fibers. In order to take advantage of, say, Canada's huge hemp production, an improvement in harvesting, fiber-stripping machinery, and retting chemistry will be needed.

People no longer call me foolish for selling hemp. Recently, I have witnessed two important attitude shifts. Around 2000, I noticed that people no longer ask me, "What is hemp? Can you smoke it?" It seems that, finally, most people understand the difference between hemp and marijuana. The second, more important change happened in 2006 when it suddenly became popular to be environmentally conscious. My business has seen a huge increase in demand for natural products like organic cotton and hemp.

As hemp's popularity grows and more products are introduced and new markets open up, hemp will take its place next to other stable farm crops such as corn, soy, cotton and wheat. Given its sustainable profile, hemp will surely be able to shed its outlaw image and become the fabric of choice for manufacturers and consumers alike.

Leather for Life

Matt Richards, Head Tanner
Rowan Gabrielle, President
Stacie Shepp, Vice President

Organic Leather
20 Sunnyside, Suite A199
Mill Valley, CA 94941
www.organicleather.com

Modern leather tanneries and the leather they make are frighteningly toxic. So toxic that there are more tanneries than any other business on the Environmental Protection Agency's (EPA) Superfund list, the list that identifies the priority environmental cleanups in the U.S. So toxic that 95 percent of U.S. tanneries have moved their operations overseas to avoid environmental oversight penalties. So toxic that many old tannery sites can't be used for agriculture or built on or even sold.

Leather-making wasn't always toxic. Ancient peoples all over the world used benign wood smoke and natural oils to make soft and durable leather very similar to today's chamois. With the advent of agriculture, bark tannage came into use. This new method yielded firmer, denser leathers, which were well suited for horse gear, hard-soled footwear, belts, and armor. Alum, a naturally occurring mineral salt, was used in many desert regions to make soft leather that retained a smooth-grain surface. As societies grew and ideas traveled, these tanning methods were combined to create leathers that met a wide variety of needs. Before plastics, leather was what you reached for when you needed something very flexible yet very strong.

In the 18th and 19th centuries, virtually every U.S. town had a tannery to meet the need for footwear, horse gear, gloves and the like. During the Industrial Revolution, manufacturing became more specialized and concentrated in various regions, but was still done with the same natural materials as before. The chief negative environmental consequence became the increased quantity of effluents being dumped into waterways.

In the 1870s, as the chemical industry grew, a new method of tanning was developed based on hexavalent and trivalent chromium (chromium (VI) and (III) respectively). By 1890, it had entered into commercial production and was quickly becoming the dominant tanning method. Quick and permanent, chrome tanning creates soft leathers, dyes easily, and lends itself nicely to mechanization. Unfortunately, the chemicals are also extremely poisonous and linger in ecosystems. In addition to chromium, modern tanneries typically use synthetic chemicals such as sodium sulphide, formaldehyde, glutaraldehyde, sulphuric acid, various solvents (which release volatile organic compounds), bactericides, paints, dyes, degreasers and surfactants.

In the late 20th century, the tanning industry's heavy use of chemicals came under intense scrutiny. The reaction of the leather industry has taken three forms: lobbying the EPA to relax rules or to not implement them, moving tanneries offshore—primarily to China and India—where there are no (or less stringent) environmental rules, and mitigating and cleaning the effluent that they do create. While this last effort is a measurable improvement over past practices, many worrisome toxins cannot be completely eradicated and still constitute a huge problem. As a result, the tanning industry all but disappeared in the U.S. Most remaining operations focus on the finishing (re-tanning, dyeing and softening) of hides that are chrome tanned off shore.

Chromium (VI) is the most persistent toxin used by the leather industry. It is a known carcinogen with the following documented human health effects:

• Skin rashes

• Upset stomachs and ulcers

• Respiratory problems

• Weakened immune systems

• Kidney and liver damage

- Alteration of genetic material

- Lung cancer

- Death

Because of these, most tanneries have switched to chromium (III), which is considerably less toxic. However, chromium (III) commonly oxidizes into chromium (VI) during the tanning process. As a result, the finished leather and the tanneries' effluent often contain chromium (VI).

Even as a compound in finished leather products, chromium (VI) causes allergic reactions such as skin rashes and ulcers, and because of its oxidized nature, it moves easily across membranes such as human skin. According to the EPA, 95 percent of all leather produced has been tanned with chromium. If you own a leather jacket, shoes composed partially or entirely of leather, a leather handbag, or leather upholstery, you can be virtually assured that it has been chrome-tanned and that you have been exposed to chromium (VI).

Natural leather is a response to consumers' increased environmental consciousness. In Europe, there is a large movement to eliminate chromium from leather, generally by replacing it with glutaraldehyde, syntans, and other metallic salts such as titanium and phosphonium. Syntans are manmade tanning agents that come in a wide variety of forms. Some are known carcinogens and environmentally hazardous, and some haven't been tested enough to know one way or another. The main advantage of these chromium substitutes is that once the tanning is done, the chemicals are bound firmly to the leather and do not pose a serious health risk to the consumer. They are, however, very dangerous to the tannery workers and to the environment.

Our brand, Organic Leather, focuses on creating high-quality and stylish leather goods as we work to transform the leather industry and educate consumers. Organic leather returns reverence to the practice of working with leather. It pays homage to tribal peoples and it encourages respect for the quality of animals' lives, from the way they are raised to the way they die. As a byproduct of the meat industry, harvesting hides and skins for leather does not encourage the killing of more animals. Rather, it makes sure that no part of the animal goes to waste. We are very concerned with the chemicals used in the tanning and dyeing processes and their effects on the natural environment and the health of both workers and customers. Because of these considerations, we have chosen the farmers and tanners that we work with very carefully, developing partnerships to create change in the leather industry.

From our experience, people who are educated about leather would prefer to wear the skin of an animal that was treated with respect; they want to minimize the amount of toxins in the water and wear a material that does not threaten their health. Of course, they also want their leather to be beautiful, supple, and strong.

Organic Leather uses three grades of leather, which we define ourselves. There are two parts to being certified organic leather. First, the animal has been raised organically, and second the tanning uses only plant and non-toxic materials. The three grades we use are:

- "Certified organic leather" comes from certified organic livestock that is then organically tanned.

- "Natural leather" comes from animals raised on small family farms that have been humanely raised but have not received organic certification, and it has also been organically tanned.

- "Naturally tanned wild harvested leathers" come from wild game animals, such as deer, that are hunted in a sustainable fashion and are tanned with our organic tanning process.

For the consumer to trust that the leather they are buying is truly green, and to encourage tanneries to produce truly natural leathers, it helps to have a third-party certification program. The USDA National Organic Program (NOP) certifies that an animal was raised and tanned organically. Because there are many animal skins that are naturally raised but do not qualify as organic, it would be preferable to have a certification specific to the leather tanning process.

In order to bring leather tanning back to an ecologically balanced position, we need to use natural tanning agents such as tannins, alum, earth minerals, fish oils and wood smoke. All of these are still used in modern tanning methods, albeit usually combined with chrome or other chemicals. By applying natural agents in a modern manufacturing context, we can turn the tanning industry around.

Natural tanning proceeds roughly as follows: The frozen or salted skin is rehydrated in fresh water and then soaked in a de-hairing solution, typically composed of hydrated lime and an enzyme. Next, the skin is mechanically fleshed and de-haired, and the lime is neutralized.

The skin is then soaked in whichever tanning agent will impart the desired quality of leather: alum for soft grain leathers; cod oil or wood smoke for soft, breathable, washable suede; and plant tannins, which, depending on type, create either dense, thick leathers (think belts or saddles) or soft grains and suede. Tanning agents can also be combined to achieve desirable qualities. Alum plus woodsmoke yields soft, washable grain leathers. Alum plus sumac or gambier tannins yield soft yet durable leathers that dye easily. Wood smoke plus tannins produces similar qualities but with improved washability.

After tanning, the skins can be dyed, oiled, dried and softened, and then buffed or polished. Colors readily available to the natural leather tanner include white, creams, yellows, tans, browns, reddish browns, blacks and reds, which are attained through the tanning process. Tannin-based dyes can also be used after tanning to create any of the tannin colors, without significantly changing the nature of the leather. Cochineal (a beetle that grows on prickly pear cactus and is commonly known as Carmine) makes a variety of reds and lavenders.

At the moment, our designers at Organic Leather work with a somewhat limited palette of colors, qualities and textures. The number of options will dramatically increase as the industry grows.

Natural tanning can be done using the same modern machinery employed by chemical tanning. The cost is somewhat higher because this is a small, new industry and because harsh chemicals are occasionally replaced by hand work. At this point, one significant cost entailed by the organic tanner is hide transportation. Compared to conventional ranchers, organic ranchers are few and far between, which results in the tanner having to truck smaller quantities of hides from multiple locations. The organic tanner may also need to pay a slightly higher price for the organic hides. These added costs, though significant at present, should largely come down as the organic meat industry grows.

Further costs are incurred due to the longer-than-conventional tanning process. Modern conventional tanning chemicals, such as sodium sulphide, cut the time required to soak and de-hair hides from one week to mere hours. They are so potent, they turn the hair into pulp and allow the entire de-hairing process to take place in a large spinning drum without human interference. The hides stay in the drum throughout the wet stage of the tanning process while different chemicals are added and drained out as required. The downside to this convenience is the fact that the chemical-laden pulp ends up in the sewage system, where it binds with oxygen, leaving none for the aquatic life.

Without sulphides, hides must be soaked in hydrated lime for a week until the hair can be pushed off by machine. This process is imperfect, so each hide must be inspected and de-haired by hand as needed. The longer tanning process requires considerably more capital and therefore entails more risk for the tanner. In addition, the labor cost difference is huge—but so is the environmental impact. The conventional tanning industry has spent time and money trying to remove sulphides from the de-hairing process. So far, however, it has only mitigated their use on the grounds that financial profit outweighs cost to the ecosystem.

As these examples illustrate, some organic leather tanning costs are driven up by the natural inefficiencies of scale. We expect costs to fall as the industry grows. Other costs are caused by technological failings. These may or may not be solved through research and development.

We have started working with willing tanneries in the U.S., helping to replace ones that have moved oversees or have been closed down. (We are also building fair trade partnerships with tanneries in developing nations, helping them convert from chemical to natural processes.) Because they use natural agents, our partner tanneries' waste is completely benign (it can even be shoveled onto fields as fertilizer); their workers enjoy safer conditions, and the end product is safe for the consumer. Meanwhile, the quality of the leather is not compromised. Naturally tanned leathers are beautiful and can be produced in a wide variety of thicknesses and colors, and with characteristics such as washability, breathability or water-resistance, stretchiness or firmness, drape or rigidity.

When we started this business, we asked ourselves a very important question: How do we produce a material that can be used in a beautiful design that honors the environment, that has incredible longevity and durability, and that creates a product that consumers will love? With Organic Leather, we believe we have answered this question. Leather grows and changes as you wear it, and is one of those magical materials that gets better and better with age.

Evolution Or Revolution

Michael Kininmonth, Technical Marketing Manager
Apparel Lenzing

www.lenzing.com

Historians have branded the 1800s the British century, the 1900s the American century, and predict that we are now in a time that will become known as the Chinese century. Equally, textile historians could label the 1800s as the century of natural fibers and the 1900s as that of the synthetics. The question remains: Which fibers will dominate in the 21st century?

Textile fibers can be divided into three groups:

- Natural fibers originating from plants or animals (cotton, wool or silk, for example)

- Synthetic fibers based on mineral oil (polyester, polyamide or acrylics)

- Man-made fibers based on natural sources such as wood

Synthetic fibers account for 57 percent of the global fiber production, natural fibers for 38 percent and man-made fibers for five percent. Cotton, for centuries the most important of all fibers, now takes second place to polyester. Other fibers appear relegated to little more than niche positions in a global textile market which, until now, was driven by the ready availability of cheap fossil fuels and the demand for commodity textiles.

The annual global demand for textile fibers is around 63 million tons, which represents an average per capita consumption of 9.8 kg. It is forecast that fiber demand for textiles and non-wovens will continue to grow by three to four percent per annum, triggered particularly by both the growth in population and the improved standard of living in developing and newly industrializing countries.

Is it likely, therefore, that polyester and cotton can continue their dominance? Or are there opportunities for other fibers to assert themselves? There are at least two reasonable scenarios to justify a "yes" to the latter question. One is based upon a popular management consultant's proposition from the early 1990s. It is known as the "cellulosics gap" theory, and it goes something like this:

• World population continues to grow.

• All of those people will require clothing.

• Oil is certain to become an increasingly scarce resource that will put price pressure on synthetics.

- The growing population will also need food. High-grade agricultural land is limited, which in turn limits total yield. (Yield can be increased using genetic modification, improved irrigation, pesticides, etc., but not infinitely stretched.)

- Cotton also requires high-grade land, pitting it in competition with food crops. Therefore, total cotton yields are unlikely to increase.

- By 2050, it is estimated that there will be up to 20 million tons of unmet demand for cotton and polyester.

- The difference could be met by man-made cellulosics, which can grow on land that cannot support food crops.

- In addition to their well-documented consumer comfort, aesthetic and performance benefits, cellulosic fibers also offer the potential for very attractive environmental characteristics.

- The lyocell process in particular offers an efficient and environmentally acceptable way of converting natural cellulose into premium quality fiber.

- Importantly, the process technology offers the potential to produce fiber on a scale and at a cost that can compete with cotton and polyester.

The second scenario is probably even more persuasive than the first. It starts with the fact that a textile revolution is in the air. Green fashion has come and gone over the past 20 years, but it finally seems here to stay. Concern for a sustainable future—fueled by such issues as shrinking natural resources, climate change and energy security—is real. Consumers are not interested in a passing fashion trend, and businesses need to look beyond the "quick-buck" business opportunity. The previous "nuts and berries," purist approach to environmentalism resulted in a high-priced, unattractive product. Fortunately, that is now being replaced by a much more pragmatic, commercial and practical attitude. The effects will be seen right along the supply chain, from how the manufacturers make their products to how brands and retailers source, merchandise and sell their garments. Just like any other industry in the global economy, textiles and apparel will have to adopt sustainable and responsible business practices. In the long run, they are unlikely to survive unless they are seen to be serious about the planet's future. Cellulosics can be produced sustainably, and therefore stand to gain prominence.

With more than 65 years of experience in the production of cellulosic fibers, the Lenzing Group, which is distinguished by its long-standing history of rigorous and cutting-edge environmental practices, is well placed to benefit from this revolution.

Lenzing manufactures all three generations of man-made cellulose fibers: viscose, modal and lyocell. Viscose is appreciated for its softness and water-retention. It is also considered a purer fiber and is the dominant cellulose fiber in non-woven hygiene applications. Modal, the second-generation cellulose fiber, is characterized by superior textile care properties. It can be found in high-quality lingerie and knitwear. Lyocell represents the latest generation of cellulose fibers. It is the most flexible in terms of application, being suitable for knits, wovens and non-wovens. Its unique, nano-fibrillar structure provides many unique textile properties including highly effective moisture management for superb comfort, natural bacterial suppression and next-to-skin benefits. Tencel® is the brand name for lyocell fibers produced by Lenzing.

Cellulose, which makes up all these fibers, is one of the organic substances generated from carbon and solar energy by plants during photosynthesis. Cellulose is the most important building material in nature and available in abundance. Every year, some 40 billion tons grow worldwide, of which 0.3 percent of the total cellulose is used by the pulp industry.

In a sense, the production and management of cellulose is Lenzing's business. The cellulose we use comes from wood, a renewable resource, and so our business is intimately tied with sustaining forests. In this way, Lenzing inserts itself unobtrusively into the natural carbon cycle.

In Austria, where Lenzing's pulp mill is integrated with its fiber plant, beech wood from nearby forests is used as raw material for viscose and modal. Eucalyptus from South Africa is the feedstock for lyocell production. In all cases, the wood is derived exclusively from forests that are managed sustainably, in keeping with forestry regulations. Lenzing has paid particular attention to forestry management practices when developing partnerships with wood pulp suppliers. Independent accreditation schemes, which have the support of environmental organizations such as Friends of the Earth and Greenpeace, have been adopted by Lenzing. A leading example is the Forestry Stewardship Council (FSC). It offers a labeling scheme for forest products (including wood pulp) that provides "a credible guarantee that the product comes from a well-managed forest." The Principles and Criteria of FSC cover issues such as protecting water quality, managing the effects on threatened or endangered species and monitoring the effects of harvesting techniques.

In all of their fiber manufacturing activities, Lenzing has managed to address the major environmental issues associated with the textile sector:

- Energy use

- Solid waste disposal

- Release of chemicals in waste water

- Release of gaseous components into the atmosphere

- Use of toxic chemicals (which may harm human health and the environment).

Lenzing's commitment to sustainable industrial practices can be witnessed at our main production site in

Austria, which is the largest integrated pulp and fiber production plant in the world, producing approximately 210,000 tons per annum.

Substantial efforts are made to fully utilize all parts of the tree by converting its non-cellulose constituents to value-added chemicals. An ever-growing competence in wood, cellulose and fiber chemistry is the basis for on-going research, which aims to identify new applications, additional market segments and products for promising new businesses.

About 40 percent of the tree is turned into pulp. Ten percent finds its way into resalable by-products, an example of which as xylose. This wood sugar is converted into Xylitol—a type of sugar that is a natural and healthy alternative to refined sugars and artificial sweeteners and can protect teeth against decay.

The other 50 percent of the tree is used for electrical power generation on the site. In fact, 85 percent of the on-site power generation is met by biogenic fuel sources, and fossil fuels such as oil, gas and coal are only needed to make up the 15 percent shortfall.

Viscose, modal and lyocell fibers consume a significant amount of water during their industrial processing: between 100 cubic m3/ ton for lyocell and up to 500 m3/ ton for viscose and modal. However, these figures are low compared to the amount of water used for the artificial irrigation of cotton –7,000 m3/ ton in Israel, and 29,000 m3/ ton in Sudan are just two examples.

The Lenzing manufacturing site takes all its water from the river that feeds the largest tourist lake in Austria. Thanks to the construction of a multi-stage biological waste water treatment plant, waste water is returned to the same river with a very high level of purity.

At Tencel manufacturing sites, one can witness the most environmentally responsible man-made fiber production ever practiced. The lyocell manufacturing process differs from that of other regenerated cellulosics, such as viscose, in that it proceeds without the formation of intermediate compounds and there is no curing or ripening stage. Therefore, the whole process is complete in three hours, rather than the 24 hours typically required. Shortened processing time implies savings in energy and water per unit of product. The minimal use of chemicals means that the pure cellulose pulp changes only physically rather than chemically. As a result, lyocell fiber is 100 percent biodegradable.

The production process for Tencel is characterized by an almost completely closed solvent cycle. The spinning bath is cleaned; the excess water is removed by evaporation; and the solvent is then recovered for re-use. The water generated during evaporation is used in the washing process. On account of the closed-loop process, the solvent necessary for production is recovered almost completely. The remaining small amount of emissions are treated before disposal.

Still, the most popular "environmentally friendly" fibers seem to be organic cotton or bamboo viscose. Organic cotton uses a significant amount of water and high-grade land, and produces low yields. Bamboo textiles tend to be made from bamboo pulp in old viscose plants, which may explain the presence of heavy metals in many of the fiber samples we have tested. In theory, Lenzing's know-how could be applied to using bamboo as a source of pulp, and certainly pulp supply will be important for all cellulosic man-made fiber manufacturers.

It's clear that one fiber alone cannot fulfill the breadth of textile needs either now or in the future. It's also clear that peoples' choices are influenced by misinformation and a lack of knowledge.

The facts about Tencel are irrefutable, and its status as the premium sustainable fiber is unequivocal:

- There is full transparency concerning the source of raw material stock.

- The raw material is fully sustainable.

- The fiber production route is chemically simple.

- The manufacturing process is environmentally benign.

- Tencel fibers can be converted to a very wide range of commercial textile and industrial products.

- At the end of their life, lyocell products are biodegradable.

- The products of this biodegradation can be considered as contributing to photosynthesis, and hence the growth of new trees for future lyocell production.

- The fiber production can be done on a large scale.

To apply one of the current environmental phrases, one could say that Tencel is truly a "Cradle to Cradle" product: a fiber ready to meet the environmental and commercial demands of the 21st century.

Organic Printing on an Industrial Scale

Andrew Lunt, Co-Founder,
T Shirt & Sons

11 Washington Road
West Wilts Trading Est
Westbury BA13 4JP
andy@tshirtandsons.co.uk

I'm a printer. I enjoy producing a fine print. I receive satisfaction knowing that the shirts I use are high quality. Just as I don't want to spoil a premium t-shirt with an inferior printing job, I don't want to contaminate an organic t-shirt with toxic ink.

Most of the inks used in printing today, along with the printing processes themselves, are hazardous to both the environment and to human health. When my company made the decision to become organic, we knew we would have to do our own research and develop novel ways of printing. The result of this decision was a two-and-a-half year research project, and the pride of becoming the U.K.'s first certified organic printer.

The term "organic" deserves clarification here, as it is a word that has been ruthlessly thrown around and exploited for commercial gain. The public was first introduced to this term as it applied to food, particularly to agricultural products. Initially, organic meant that only the farming techniques were regulated to protect the environment and human health. In many instances, this entailed replacing some or all of the petrochemicals used as pesticides, herbicides and fertilizers with more natural processes. Many people misunderstand the term organic to mean that no man-made chemicals may factor into the given process. In many cases, this would be impossible. As the organic food movement gained popularity, the word "organic" was slapped on any product manufacturers deemed to be beneficial to human health and the environment. Now, regulatory bodies set strict standards for what can and cannot be called organic, though the definitions of each regulatory body tend to differ slightly from one to another. As it applies to printing, the organic label regulates not only the chemicals in our inks, but also how we dispose of our waste and how we monitor our records to ensure accountability. Converting to an organic printing company entailed reevaluating our entire production system from source to finish.

We took our first step towards organic production years before applying for organic certification, when we decided to purchase organic cotton apparel. Twenty years ago, the idea of organic, fair-trade cotton had not yet occurred to our clients. When demand for an ethical piece of clothing did arrive, all we could offer was an unbleached t-shirt. Today, the socially and environmentally conscious consumer has come of age, and we now have requests for "harvest to high street" organic production. In other words, the customer wants to be sure that his or her apparel has been treated according to organic guidelines at every stage of its production.

Sadly, there just isn't enough organic cotton to go around at the moment, despite the obvious advantages to farmers. Demand for organic cotton has developed faster than farms can transition from conventional to fully-certified organic cultivation. As a result, the price of organic cotton has shot up. Speculators snap up the year's harvest as soon as it hits the markets, which further drives up the price. Even though this boom is good for growers, inevitably it makes organic garments more expensive once they hit the street and risks alienating certain customers. Hopefully, the supply of organic cotton will catch up to demand as more and more cotton farmers realize the economic and environmental advantages of transition.

Due to the limited supply of organic cotton, we print on both organic and non-organic cotton. We figure that a cleanly printed conventional t-shirt is better than a toxically printed conventional t-shirt. Switching between t-shirt types does not prevent our process from qualifying as organic. As long as we ensure not a single fiber from a non-organic shirt is left on a machine that prints on organic shirts, we are within the standards.

Once we identified and committed to suppliers for organic cotton, we looked at the next step in production: the actual printing of the t-shirt. Ink is the crucial component of this process. First, we researched all inks containing hazardous chemicals—which were just about all of them! This was not a good sign. In printing, one of the main culprits is PVC, or polyvinyl chloride, which is found in 30 to 50 percent of all plastisol (oil-based) inks. Plastisol inks are user friendly in that they do not dry out, and do not require a solvent. However, the presence of PVC is an important concern because that polymer contains phthalates, chemical substances that persist in the environment and have been linked to cancer.

Many companies advertise their use of water-based inks. This encourages consumers to mistakenly believe that these inks are safer than their plastisol counterparts. Needless to say, the industry does nothing to correct the public's perception. In fact, water-based inks typically use water as a solvent along with co-solvents containing synthetic chemicals that shorten drying time. Actually, most water-based inks are no safer than their plastisol counterparts. Using them responsibly requires taking strenuous precautions in handling and waste disposal. Few printers can be bothered.

To develop safe, effective alternatives to plastisol-based inks, we teamed up with the chemists at the ink manufacturer with whom we already had a strong relationship. Persuading the manufacturer to develop new ink formulas took persistence. We eventually convinced them that organic t-shirt printing was a new market that could be developed. Two-and-a-half years later, we declared the ink problem solved! We now use a safe, water-based ink that leaves no residue in the finished product that could be absorbed through the skin. Actually, we haven't invented anything entirely new. We've merely done our research and turned up an existing formula whose benefits are numerous. Quality has improved and our printed shirts are extremely soft to the touch after countless washings. Oil-based prints tend to be brittle and crack.

Aromatic solvents are also vital to the process of getting pigments to bind to the fabric. The organic standards, therefore, don't forbid their use. However, they do require that technical grade aromatic solvents be used instead of "white spirit." White spirit is a broad term that often refers to the cheapest, least pure aromatic solvents. A technical grade aromatic solvent is much purer (and more expensive) than what's needed to get the printing job done, but it is necessary to maintain a clean, environmentally conscious shop. And the work environment is improved. Our workers no longer need to wear bulky protective gear. They could literally wash their hands in the dye if they wanted!

We didn't stop there. After resolving the ink issue, we examined all aspects of our production to identify opportunities for improvement. Since we were deter-mined to remove any non-organic process from our factory, we monitored all our waste and trade effluent. T-shirt printing uses a lot of water (for washing down screens, among other things). We keep the water con-taminate-free through a system of chemistry, filters and holding tanks. Pea gravel removes the insoluble stuff. If we use an acid to remove the emulsion, then we use an alkali to bring the pH values below the limit proscribed by the water authority. The water then neutralizes in holding tanks before going down the drain. We pay to have our ink, considered industrial waste, taken away by a third party. The same com-pany also takes away our rags for cleaning once a month, exchanging them for clean ones.

Soon we realized that some sort of benchmark needed to exist in order for this evolution to have any credibility and meaning. Accordingly, we approached the Soil Association, the organization responsible for certifying organic food production in the U.K. They showed an interest in our company, as they were get-ting more inquiries from both retail and from gar-ment manufacturers to license finished, 100 percent organic, printed clothing. At the time, there was no licensed printer, so only "blank" garments were able to carry the Soil Association mark.

We applied to the Soil Association in February 2006. After months of discussion, some last-minute tweaks in our production and factory inspections, we were awarded certification. When the global organic cotton standard is developed, we anticipate being the first to produce a fully-licensed printed organic t-shirt.

While I strongly believe any business with enough determination can become organic, I admit that

T Shirt & Sons has the advantage of scale. Our company prints tens of thousands of shirts per week and caters to large, socially conscious clients like Friends of the Earth and Greenpeace. A smaller printer may not have been able to put up the same amount of time and money we did. Although converting to organic proved intensive, I believe it will pay off in both reputation and profit. We are already experiencing an increase in efficiency as the result of reevaluating our production methods. One year after our organic certification, the volume of our business is more than twice what it was in the previous year.

Another unforeseen benefit has arisen from the meticulous tracking required under the organic certification rules. If in five years a customer comes to me with a serial number, I should be able to give him the exact pigments used in its batch. Never have we been so aware of our production methods, letting us quickly identify and eliminate a great deal of waste.

Our early investment makes us feel confident of a long and prosperous future, as demand for organic products will only increase. Manufacturers must anticipate this demand and meet it now with their own investments and initiatives. While being the world's only organic printer feels comfortable, we welcome a little healthy competition to keep us on our toes and to benefit the printing industry as a whole.

T Shirt & Sons has always believed that more could be done to lessen the carbon footprint of our product.

We are conscious of our responsibility to our customers, to our workers, and to the world. We have tried very hard to improve every aspect of the supply chain without compromising the finished product. We now have a chance to change the way we produce fashion and set a blueprint for the future. The demand is out there. It is up to businesses to respond to it.

SECTION 3:

CHANGING THE CYCLE
OF FASHION

A Clean Start

Jason Wentworth, Owner
Washboard Eco Laundry

207 Danforth Street
Portland, ME 04102
www.washboardecolaundry.com

I grew up in your typical organic-farming, solar power-using, alternatively educated, recycling, bike-riding, anti-consumer, community-activist family. With this counter-culture background, it was natural for me to focus my professional life on saving the environment. Toward that end, at the age of twenty-three, I was elected to the Maine House of Representatives. I served two terms before concluding that environmental advocates were not making better progress, in part because we were viewing the private sector as the problem rather than as an opportunity. So I walked away from the halls of power—where I had little of it—and set out to create a "green business" that would be a force for positive change.

My quest to become an "eco-entrepreneur" began without investment capital, a solid business plan or actual private sector experience. All I had was an abundance of naïve enthusiasm and a half-dozen ideas for businesses that I wished existed in my little city of Portland, Maine. These included a food waste composting company, a demolition debris recycling facility and an electric car rental business. After several relapses back into the public sector and an unfulfilling attempt to realize someone else's entrepreneurial dream of an alternative energy company, I began my current project: an eco-laundromat.

If I had known at the outset that I was about to join one of the least creative, least innovative industries in the world, I might have stayed in the solar energy business. What got me interested in laundry is the huge amount of water, electricity and gas wasted in the simple process of cleaning clothes. There are more than 30,000 laundromats in the U.S., and their collective contribution to air and water pollution and greenhouse gas emissions adds up. The more I investigated, the more motivated I became to create a new model for the laundry industry—one based on energy efficiency, environmental stewardship and social responsibility, three principles alien to the typical American laundromat. On a very personal level, I also wanted to make a nice place to do laundry. Most laundromats in our area are so dull and dingy that they make the drudgery of laundry seem like torture.

In May of 2002, with the unshakable support of my wife and a convenient home equity loan, I bought an existing laundromat business that was figuratively and literally on the verge of falling into the basement. The location offered a neighborhood with lots of apartments, and an historic building with a south-facing roof and great potential hidden behind a ghastly 1980s-era renovation.

From May until November, we ran the business more or less as we found it: we lost money and attracted only those customers who couldn't easily travel to one of the two closest competitors. During this time, we got to know the neighborhood and the potential customer base, and to plan the renovation that began in early November.

I had four initial goals for the renovation: select the most energy-efficient and durable machines; use as many low-impact, local materials as possible in the construction process; incorporate a solar hot water system; and create a space that is inviting, comfortable and healthy. With my experience in alternative energy and green building, and my wife's excellent sense of design, all this seemed easy enough to accomplish. It quickly became obvious that we had a great deal to learn about how the laundry industry functions, and how the reality of running a small business gets in the way of great ideals. Our first hurdle was not having any model to follow. I was unable to find any existing laundromats that were doing all the things that we wanted to do with ours. Moreover, most of the laundry "experts" I talked to were not encouraging at all. In fact, every laundry equipment sales person tried to convince me that energy efficiency was not very important, assured me solar was unreliable and a waste of money, and suggested that my store should look nearly identical to that of my most successful competitor. I was on my own!

By far the greatest challenge I faced was selecting the washers and dryers. Things have changed significantly in the past five years, but at the time I began my search none of the five major companies I talked to published information on how many total gallons of water their washers used per cycle, or how many watts of electricity they required per load. They could tell me the voltage requirements, hot water and gas consumption, and peak amp loads because those figures are needed to size the electric and gas service and water heater(s). However, these numbers do not give an accurate picture of total machine efficiency. For that, I had to talk with the design engineers. In the end, we settled on front-loading washers that use about 50 percent less water and electricity than the typical top-loading machines seen in most laundromats. These washers also have an extract (final spin) speed about five times faster than most commercial units. This means the clothes come out with a very low humidity level, cutting drying time by about 35 percent. Not surprisingly, these washers are made within the European Union, which has enacted high-efficiency standards for both commercial and residential appliances. Few options existed on the drying side, but we were able to find units that had fairly low gas and electric consumption compared to the average laundromat dryer.

Before the machines could be installed, we had to completely gut and rebuild a 1,100 square foot space that was originally constructed around 1906. We were able to save the roof, tin ceiling, sub floor and wall framing, but everything else needed to be replaced. The overhaul gave us the chance to make some significant, energy-saving improvements and also to transform the store into a very pleasant place to do laundry.

We installed 22 new, insulated windows (only two windows, both inoperable, existed before) that created excellent natural lighting, ventilation, and allowed for good solar gain in the winter. These windows obviate the need for air conditioning in the summer, cut our electric lighting needs by half during the day, and make the general atmosphere more enjoyable for customers and employees. We also replaced all the fluorescent tube fixtures with compact fluorescent lights. Stylish, high efficiency fixtures simultaneously improved the quality of lighting and, together with the windows, cut the operating cost by more than 70 percent. A two-inch thick, dyed concrete slab serves as the finished floor and also provides thermal mass for the efficient operation of our radiant floor heating system. It is fed by the same 95 percent efficient natural gas water heater that serves the washers. A special variance from the plumbing inspector to use the same unit for both purposes was required to do this. It was worth it; we reduced our capital costs and simplified the entire heating system.

For the first time in the building's history, insulation was installed. We used low-impact cellulose in the ceiling and fiberglass batts in the walls, achieving an insulation level of R11 in the walls and R40 in the ceiling (ratings that well exceed those of typical commercial buildings).

In our public bathroom, we installed low-flow toilet and sink fixtures and a waterless urinal. Plumbing was upgraded to create the shortest runs possible for hot water delivery to the washers. All the piping was insulated. Recycling stations set up throughout the store recover plastic, glass, paper, cardboard, metals and clothing. The soda machine was removed and replaced with an Energy Star-rated mini-fridge, allowing us to continue selling cold beverages while cutting electrical consumption by more than $45 per month. Insulated doors were installed to cover the air intake vents for the dryers during cold winter nights when the machines are not in use. An alarm system was installed that allows all the lights to be turned off at night without sacrificing security.

Throughout the renovation, we used many local and recycled materials, avoided products with toxic components wherever possible and tried to reduce waste at each step in the process. Among them are: locally milled, sustainably harvested lumber for the siding, wall framing and trim work, recycled lumber and wheat board for the folding tables, checkout counter and center island between the machines, natural linoleum for the table and counter surfaces, low

VOC paints for the interior and exterior walls, ceiling and trim, recycled plumbing pipes and gas lines for more than 75 percent of the installation, recycled content wallboard, restored tin ceiling, and recycling more than 90 percent of the construction waste generated during the demolition and rebuilding process.

Ironically, the first thing that got me interested in this business—using solar-heated water for the washers—had to wait to be installed until later in the first year of operation. We were able to pre-plumb the system in the original renovation, but budget overruns necessitated waiting a few months before we could install the solar panels on the roof and construct the storage tank. In the fall of 2003, we were able to purchase evacuated tube collectors and build a 300-gallon storage tank in the basement. This supplements our hot water production and meets about 50 percent of our annual demand with clean, free energy from the sun.

Not only did these changes save resources and therefore money, they also contributed to our achieving an attractive and healthy space. With lots of natural ventilation, low-toxicity materials and a dust and mold free radiant floor heating system, we have high indoor air quality. Natural lighting, warm colors on the walls and floor, and a machine layout that preserves clean sight lines make the space welcoming, visually interesting and calming. We added cushioned chairs instead of the usual hard plastic seats, a bulletin board, current magazines and a wide variety of music. In a bold challenge to orthodox laundromat stricture, we did not add a TV. Though there are 21 TVs in the laundromat that was recently selected by an industry trade group as "America's Most Progressive Laundromat for 2006," our customers tell us they appreciate that we are TV-free.

We reopened the renovated eco-laundry on January 2nd, 2003 to a long line of intrigued customers. Pleased with the response to our first round of renovations, we began changing the way we operated the laundry. Our goal was to further reduce the environmental impact of the business.

One of the first steps we took was to offer several types of natural detergents that have no petroleum-based ingredients and are not tested on animals. As customers familiarized themselves with these products and our confidence grew, we eliminated some of the "brand name" detergents we sold. First, we replaced the chemical fabric softener with a product made from plant extracts. We got zero customer complaints. Next, we traded chlorine bleach for sodium percarbonate, which has extremely low toxicity and is a very effective bleaching agent. Again, only customer approval. We have also stopped stocking the little boxes of soap found in most laundromats. Instead, products are sold from bulk containers in reusable cups (sized properly for our different washers). This arrangement has helped us significantly reduce packaging and soap waste.

Two years ago, we began offering an alternative to chemical dry cleaning. We have always had a drop-off service for our customers, and for the first two years we used a contractor who did conventional dry cleaning. Yet it always made us uncomfortable to think about our customers' delicate clothes being soaked in a carcinogenic petrochemical. Fortunately, we found a local cleaner who was experimenting with "wet cleaning," a process that cleans garments using water and biodegradable detergent in a sophisticated washer. We teamed up with them to offer this service to our customers and began marketing it in the store in December of 2004. Within weeks, more than 75 percent of our customers had switched over to wet cleaning. We doubled our drop-off business in the first year and doubled it again in the second year. Our experience gave our contractor the confidence to offer the process in all of their locations, and they are starting to see the same results as ours.

The simplest operational change we made was to variably price our washers. Our machines allow us to charge twenty-five cents more for warm than for cold, fifty cents more for hot, and seventy-five cents more for "superwash" (this entails hot water and an additional rinse). Customers have a cash incentive to use a lower water temperature. As a result, we have reduced our hot water consumption by about 30 percent without restricting customer choice—people simply pay more for a more resource intensive choice.

When I tell the story of our eco-laundry one of the first questions I get is, "How well is it working?"

which often is code for, "Is it profitable?" For me there are two ways to answer this question.

By traditional business standards, our model has been a solid success. At a time when more than half of U.S. laundromats have seen their market share shrinking due to more people owning homes and buying washers and dryers, we grew by 250 percent in our first four years. Our utility costs comprise about 13 percent of gross revenue. According to a 2006 industry study, this figure is 13 percent lower than the average U.S. laundromat. Our employee retention rate is very high, particularly for an industry that provides mostly low-wage, low-skill jobs with no future for advancement. We've developed an extremely loyal customer base that does nearly all of our marketing by word of mouth. We've also had several unsolicited offers to buy the business, and one proposal to join in a partnership with a well-established professional cleaner.

I prefer to evaluate the success of the business in a non-traditional way, using a standard of sustainability that places equal value on our accomplishments in environmental stewardship, social responsibility and net return. This "triple bottom line" approach is well established in the socially-responsible business movement, but exceedingly rare in the laundry industry.

By this more holistic standard, our eco-laundry is doing very well. We are able to pay our employees a living wage, and offer paid personal time and performance bonuses that give employees a stake in the financial success of the company. In the near future, we are hoping to add a health insurance benefit. Our prices for washing and drying are slightly lower than the competition, a real value to many of our customers who live paycheck to paycheck. The store features a free clothes area where we put out items left behind for people in need to take. Moreover, we regularly sponsor fundraising events to help support local non-profit groups.

Our focus on energy efficiency has reduced our greenhouse gas emissions at the same time as the business has grown. So far, we have avoided generating more than one and a half million gallons of wastewater and saved nearly 3,000 gallons of detergent. Through our aggressive recycling program, we produce only one 15-gallon bag of trash per week and recover about 50 gallons of unused detergent annually. We continue our improvement efforts by developing a heat recovery system for our dryers and expanding our bicycle delivery service, and are planning to buy wind power as soon as it becomes available for small businesses in our area.

Most rewarding is the customer and community response. We get positive reinforcement daily. This has convinced me of something I hoped would be true when I started this venture; people understand the importance of developing a new economy that serves human needs in a sustainable way. A business that is based on environmental and social responsibility will get the customer support needed to succeed.

———∞∞∞———

The Environmental Impact of Laundry

Elizabeth P. Easter, Professor
Department of Merchandising, Apparel and
Textiles

The School of Human Environmental Sciences
University of Kentucky
Lexington, KY 40506

In the beginning, there were streams and rocks for cleaning, and fresh air and sunshine for drying. Then a scrub board and wash tub or kettle allowed women (usually) to do laundry nearer to home. Freeing a family's clothes of soil, stains and smells took the better part of the day and a lot of elbow grease. The Industrial Revolution brought the wringer washer machine: a simple tub on legs, with a hand crank-operated wringer on top. This mitigated the onerous task of twisting out moisture in preparation for drying and enjoyed a good 50 years of consumer devotion until, in the early 1950s, households embraced automatic clothes washers. Although new cycles and buttons have been added since then, automatic washers today

have the same basic parts as they did then: a perforated double tub with an agitator in the center to
move the clothes through a water bath. We also
have mechanized laundry drying, whereby hot air
is blown through spinning perforated tubs.
Americans consider their washers and dryers time-
saving necessities; however, collectively these
appliances utilize vast quantities of water and
energy. The good news is, as a result of industry
competition and government mandates to reduce
energy usage in the past ten years, laundry products have become more energy efficient.

There are several opportunities to reduce water and
energy usage during laundering. Currently, 75–85
percent of all washers sold in the U.S. are vertical axis
(VA) washers with a central agitator. (You may also
hear these referred to as top-loading washers.) Most
VA washers suspend the clothes in a tub of water for
washing and rinsing, a process that typically requires
about 40 gallons of water per load. Forty gallons may
seem insignificant in the larger scheme of water
usage, but approximately 35 billion loads of laundry
are washed annually in the United States.

About ten years ago, the majority of U.S. appliance
manufacturers began to offer high-efficiency (HE)
clothes washers that come in two basic designs.
Horizontal axis (HA) models (also called front-loading machines) tumble clothing through a small bath
of water. Modified VA machines combine low-post
or no-post agitators with spray washes and rinses.

Both of these technologies avoid immersing the clothes in a tub of water, with the result that they use as little as 20–60 percent of the water that a conventional VA machine does.

Clearly, water needs to be conserved for its own sake, but, conveniently enough, it turns out that saving water also translates into saving energy. In his 2004 final project report for the Department of Energy titled Energy Efficient Laundry Process, Tim Richter concluded that approximately 50 percent of all energy consumed during the laundry process is expended heating water. The other half is required for the controls and to power the motor for spin and agitation. Due to the reduction in water, HE washer energy can amount to as little as 20–50 percent of that used by VA washers.

Simply lowering water temperature also reduces energy usage. Historically, to enable sanitation as well as cleaning, "hot" water temperatures ranged from 160°–212° F. Today, most washers offer sanitization as an option, but boiling-hot water has not been standard since the early 1990s, when household water heaters were mandated to leave the manufacturer with a pre-set of no more than 120° (in large part to reduce the danger of scalding burns for children). With the ceiling lowered, manufacturers soon dropped the temperatures corresponding to their "warm" and "cold" labels as well. Consumers didn't mind: a reduction from 160° to 120° saved them money. In addition, installing a built-in heater, an idea imported to the U.S. from Europe, allows one to heat just enough water for washing rather than the entire 75-gallon household tank.

The advent of automatic temperature control systems allowed water temperature to be precisely controlled. Prior to this, inefficiencies used to result from day-to-day temperature variation of the water in the pipes. In the winter, cold (unheated) water could be 40°; in the summer, it could reach 60°. As a consequence, the person who selected cold water on the dial in winter and in summer would actually be treating their clothes very differently, and the person who selected warm water in winter and in summer would not require the same mix of hot and cold water to achieve the desired temperature. Automatic control systems both ensure consistent washing conditions and limit the amount of hot water needed.

In parallel to mechanical developments, consumer habits regarding washing temperature are also changing. Studies have shown that consumers do significantly fewer loads in hot water. Less than ten percent of all clothes loads are washed in hot water. The apparel industry may also be given credit for this trend. Today, most care labels recommend washing in either warm or cold water. As a matter of fact, care labels specifying hot water are few and far between. In a 2006 study, Deena Cotterill compiled the information on care labels of over 1,831 consumer garments and home furnishings. Only four recommended hot water, while 62 percent recommended cold water. The industry trend to recommend a colder water temperature is based on the premise that fabrics may shrink less and colors remain vibrant in colder water.

The DOE measures washer efficiency using the Modified Energy Factor (MEF). As of January 1, 2007, all washing machines sold in the United States must comply with a revised MEF of 1.26. The MEF is an energy efficiency metric that corresponds to the washer capacity in cubic feet divided by the total energy consumption per cycle in kWh. Total energy consumption takes into account the energy to run the washer (motors and controls), the energy to heat the water, and the energy used by the dryer to remove moisture from the clothes. In regards to energy usage, the higher the MEF, the more energy efficient the clothes washer. Reduced water temperatures and increased spin speed significantly impact MEF.

The DOE has also created the Energy Star® Program, which qualifies clothes washers that meet even higher MEF numbers than the 1.26 standard. As of January 1, 2007 an Energy Star-rated washer must have: a capacity equal to or greater than 1.6 cubic feet; a MEF of 1.72 or higher; and a water factor (WF) of 8.0 or lower. The WF is a water efficiency metric that corresponds to the total weighted water consumption of the washer in gallons per cycle divided by the clothes washer capacity in cubic feet. With regards to water usage, the lower the WF, the more water efficient the clothes washer. WF mostly depends on the fundamental washing and rinsing design of the washer. In HE washers, a lower WF is obtained by reducing the quantity of water for both wash and rinse cycles.

The Energy Star label tells the consumer that the product provides significant energy savings over other energy-compliant products. According to the latest national retail sales data (through May 2006), Energy Star-qualified washers now account for 38 percent of all clothes washer sales in the United States. Qualified clothes washers are available in both HA and VA configurations. As of January 2005, 172 out of 464 washers currently in the marketplace qualified for the Energy Star. Twenty different manufacturers currently produce Energy Star washers; all leading manufacturers offer numerous models. However, as already noted, new Energy Star qualification requirements significantly changed on January 1, 2007, and the percentage of Energy Star clothes washers to total clothes washer sales will also change.

To accelerate markets for HE washers, the DOE, under its Energy Star Program and in cooperation with Maytag Appliances, conducted a field evaluation of HE washers using Bern, Kansas as a test bed. The High-Efficiency Laundry Metering and Marketing Analysis (THELMA) project developed information for promoting efficient clothes washers that use less energy and water. The research agenda of the THELMA project included lab testing, qualitative and quantitative consumer research, and in-home metering of conventional and HA machines. The hypothesis—that a changeover from conventional, VA washers to the high-efficiency, HA design would decrease water and energy consumption—was substantiated. Furthermore, it was found that decreased water consumption also yielded a decrease in the amount of wastewater produced.

The criteria used to establish the 2007 Energy Star requirements were designed to protect the value of the Energy Star brand and to ensure its continued relevance in the marketplace. However, a successful Energy Star program should not compromise the functionality or performance of the clothes washer. The Clothes Care Research CenterTM (CCRC), an alliance of leading manufacturers and research laboratories dedicated to improving clothes care in the home, expressed concern that the DOE lacked a strategy to evaluate the impact of Energy Star washers on consumer clothes loads. Their study investigated how the new DOE requirements for water and energy savings would affect consumer satisfaction regarding laundry process.

One question asked by CCRC was: If the water level is reduced, will the consumer see an effect in the appearance and/or performance of their clothes? The CCRC found that reducing water usage does not affect the appearance factors of color retention, fuzzing, pilling and smoothness. This was the case regardless of apparel construction and/or fiber content. However, reduced water usage did increase the potential for dye transfer, as measured by adding white fabrics to a typical dark colors load. Obviously, this is not typical or recommended consumer practice, but it does suggest that dye transfer may become an issue as washer manufacturers continue to minimize water usage. After all, it is not so uncommon that a white gym sock gets mixed up with darks during laundry.

The second question addressed by the study was: Will a reduction in the temperature of the wash impact the performance of the washer on typical clothes loads? Based on the results of this study, lowering the washing temperature from warm (90°F) to cold (70°F) does not affect color retention, fuzzing and pilling, or soil redeposition. However, warm water was more effective than cold or very cold water at releasing stains. Additionally, lowering the washing temperature to 60°F did adversely affect color retention and smoothness. Colors darkened or deepened, and clothes were more wrinkled. This result requires further investigation to determine the reasons.

Drying and washing should be considered together when assessing the energy efficiency of laundering. In North America, most people tumble dry their clothes. The amount of remaining moisture (measured as RMC) in the clothes after the final spin cycle in the washer must be removed by evaporation in the dryer. Research studies report that 40 percent of the total energy consumed during the laundry process is used to heat the air during drying. According to some researchers, the most effective way to improve energy efficiency in the clothes dryer is to extract as much water as possible in the washing machine. The Energy Efficient Laundry Process found that removing water during the spin cycle removes moisture at lower cost than during time-intensive water removal by the tumble action of the dryer. Accordingly, appliance manufacturers have introduced higher spin cycle speeds, which can leave the clothes with 10–15 percent less moisture. The DOE has long recognized the energy-saving potential of lower RMC. The 1994 energy standard calculated energy used during drying into the energy metric for washing machines.

The Energy Efficient Laundry Process report identifies one more thing that could save drying energy: reducing excessive dry times. The report concludes that traditional clothes dryers are not effective in controlling the appropriate duration of the drying period. Advanced control algorithms and sensor implementations are needed to determine when clothes are just dry and promptly stop the machine. New sensor technology and dryer controls are designed to improve the sensing mechanisms of the clothes load. Not only do these cutting-edge dryers provide energy savings but, as an added benefit, they prevent delicate clothing from being damaged by too much heat.

Properly considered, laundry appliances and chemistry are one system, rather than two individual entities from two industry sectors. Therefore, for an HE laundry system to reach its full potential, it must include both HE machines and HE detergents. HE is necessary to fulfill two purposes: first, to accommodate the enhanced machinery; and second, to act on clothes more efficiently.

It is well known that water extraction can be affected by chemistry. Small pores and channels in the fibers create large capillary forces that cannot be overcome by the centrifugal forces of the spin cycle. A prime driver of capillary action is water surface. Chemical additives can reduce this. Procter & Gamble explored chemical additives that would enable faster evaporation rates in the dryer and increase moisture extraction in the washer. Silicone, an additive to the detergent formulation, has been shown to reduce RMC by over 20 percent.

Recently, HE detergents have been specially formulated for the HE machines. HE machines require a detergent that can accommodate lower water levels and altered washer design. For example, the tumbling action of the HE machines generates more suds than a traditional VA. Also, the reduced water usage creates a higher concentration of detergent and soil per load. HE detergents contain suds-controlling chemicals as well as soil-suspending polymers that prevent soils and dyes from re-depositing onto clothes.

Advances in laundry chemistry have also created effective low-temperature detergents to support the reduction in hot water. In their promotion of Cold

Water Tide, P&G claims that the consumer can get hot water results in cold water, allowing him or her to save up to 80 percent of the heating cost in each load.

Although the current market for HE clothes washers is small, it is growing. As of 2005, sales of HE washers had grown from less than one percent to more that 15 percent of the market in only 10 years. This is encouraging. Nevertheless, HE washing machines face two major challenges in the marketplace: cost and consumer awareness. An HE machine does cost more than a conventional one, and this difference is not likely to significantly improve with increased demand as HE washers utilize inherently higher-cost technologies. Also, few consumers are aware of the technology and its cleaning performance, reduced operating cost, water use and energy consumption. As a conscquence, the industry finds it difficult to market and sell appliances solely on energy efficiency. Instead, it opts to sell HE washers on the strength of their options, capacity and aesthetics. Only when appliances can "pay for themselves" are buyers swayed by the energy-saving (i.e. money-saving) potential. Luckily, utility companies have provided some support by offering consumers rebates on HE washer purchases. As the market for HE laundry systems increases, however, the consumer will benefit directly by the long-term cost savings of water and energy that will translate to a significant long-term environmental benefit.

From My Closet to Africa: The Dirt on Post-Consumer Recycling

Jana Hawley, Professor and Department Head
Apparel, Textiles, and Interior Design

Kansas State University
224 Justin Hall
Manhattan, KS 66506

While performing the annual ritual of cleaning out my closets—sorting both worn and still-tagged clothing for Goodwill, consignment shops, and storage—I'm horrified by the knee-deep piles of clothing rejected for being outdated, the wrong size, stained or damaged: a summer dress from last season, a pair of jeans with a broken zipper, even the negligee from my wedding night. How did my closets become so overcrowded? Perhaps my position as a professor of fashion prompts me to maintain a certain "look," necessitating a fully stocked, up-to-date wardrobe. Or perhaps I am simply a typical American.

In the United States, we consume 83.9 pounds of textiles per person per year. That's up from 63 pounds per person five years ago. Those figures do take into consideration non-apparel textiles such as carpet, but over the same period, carpet sales have actually decreased, which leaves us to safely attribute the increase to a rise in clothing purchases. Modern homes have closets on average 60 percent larger than homes in the 1960s. What is bought today gets discarded tomorrow. According to a report issued by the Environmental Protection Agency in 2003, the per capita daily disposal rate of solid waste in the United States is approximately 4.3 pounds, up from 2.7 pounds in 1960. Regardless of how dynamic or economically viable the modern fashion industry is, it is creating a gross overabundance of used clothing, releasing a plethora of stuff into the waste management stream. The good news is, because textiles are nearly 100 percent recyclable, this potential landfill disaster can be averted.

The bad news is, textile recyclers and waste management companies could be more effective if more people were aware of what they do and their potential to do even more. The textile recycling industry is one of the oldest and most established recycling industries in the world. Yet, in general, few people understand this "hidden" industry, its players or its reclaimed textile products. I have done research on textile recycling since 1999, exploring the cycle of clothing consumption from purchase to disposal to rebirth. This fascinating topic allows me to bring social meaning to an analysis of global systems.

Textile recycling can be classified as either pre-con-sumer or post-consumer waste; a textile recycling company removes this waste from the waste stream and recycles it back into the market (both industrial and end-consumer). Pre-consumer waste consists of by-product materials from the textile, fiber, and cot-ton industries that are re-manufactured into products for the automotive, aeronautic, home building, furni-ture, paper, apparel and other industries. Post-con-sumer waste has been purchased and worn (or not—as in my things that still had the tags on them) by the consumer. I am especially interested in the post-con-sumer waste sector of the recycling industry.

The post-consumer textile recycling process com-prises myriad players, from consumers who sell their castoffs at garage sales or flea markets, to charities such as Goodwill Industries and Salvation Army, to for-profit recycling companies, to manufacturers who develop value-added products by grinding used fiber, to policymakers in the U.S. and developing countries, to savvy Japanese "pickers" who crave vin-tage Americana such as frayed Grateful Dead t-shirts or the perfectly ripped pair of faded Levis.

In the U.S. alone, this industry consists of roughly 3,000 mostly small businesses that together divert more than one and a half million tons of post-con-sumer textile waste annually. The largest and longest established companies are stable and have an established network of global accounts where used goods can be marketed. Many of the smaller or newer recyclers see textile recycling as an easy business to get into, but then fail because they lack the global network necessary for market trading. While some companies specialize in exports to developing countries, other companies have found niches in transforming used clothing into value-added products such as wipers, chair pads, casket liners, cement fill and pet bed stuffing. In Europe, where fuel costs are much higher, some of the unwearable used clothing is even pelletized and burned. Their BTU and emissions levels are really quite respectable, even with a synthetic/natural textile blend; certainly, they are much better than those yielded by burning tires, a relatively common practice in America. Unfortunately, when I was exploring the possibility of bringing this technology to the University of Missouri, where I was previously a professor, I discovered that U.S. boiler systems are built differently than European ones. They allow more air in, which would incinerate pellets too quickly.

Textile recycling companies are strategically located throughout North America to reduce trucking costs. Many of the companies are located in urban areas (Los Angeles, New York, Toronto) where there is an abundance of used clothing; however, one of the largest recycling companies in the country is MidWest Textiles in El Paso, Texas.

MidWest Textiles receives a semi-tractor load of used clothing every day. This is then emptied onto a conveyer belt and sorted into approximately 400 categories, from bed sheets, to winter coats, to summer dresses. Highly trained sorters mine for certain high-value items, particularly vintage pieces. Thom Paxton, head of the vintage division of Midwest Textiles, has an MFA and a talent for understanding what's cool or the next fashion craze. Few really great pieces are found in the truckloads that arrive but "diamonds in the rough" fetch a hefty price on the Japanese market, from a SoHo retailer, on eBay, or on the Paris auction block. One recycler from St. Louis claims that he has pulled enough valuable jeans from his conveyor to pay for his children's college.

After sorting, the clothes are baled, and then ware-housed until orders for certain goods arrive. Maybe a broker in Sri Lanka wants a 1,000-pound bale of cotton shirts for disaster relief. Or an Italian account orders a bale of assorted acrylic (or wool or cashmere) sweaters to be mutilated back to the fiber stage and made into blankets. Or perhaps an American company asks for a mixed bale to chop up to make into non-woven casket padding liners.

Bales of used clothes are much needed for the poorest in the world. While the clothing traditions of local people still exist, American and European clothing castoffs, mitumba or salaula (Kiswahili and Bemba, respectively), are very much a part of the African landscape. They provide business opportunities for some and inexpensive clothing for many, with the rather unfortunate consequence that Western styles overwhelm native garments on the street, if not yet in ceremonial situations.

Some would ask that since our used clothing often starts as a charitable donation, why not export our used clothing to Africa for free? The answer is that Africa simply does not want to take all that we throw away. Africa is a different market, not just a dumping ground, and that continent's people need to be served with the specific supply that meets their demands. For-profit recyclers separate out what they know will sell. Clearly, Africans have no use for heavy coats. Most Africans also disdain skimpy tops and mini-skirts (tradition often prohibits women from baring themselves as much as they do in the West). Men's clothing fetches a higher price than women's clothing (women tend to retain native dress longer than the men). Shirts sell not because of their designer label, but because of their bright colors or more appropriate sizes (Africans have much smaller waists, in general, than our well-fed American population). By carefully sorting and selling our used clothing to the closely established networks that have been honed over the generations, entrepreneurship has been established; the appropriate clothing is shipped to Africa; and her people are clothed at a cost that is fair.

Individuals should be encouraged to donate their clothing to their favorite charity rather than throw it away. Charities will agree, though, that the supply far exceeds the demand, and they must offload much of it onto for-profit textile recycling companies. In Columbia, Missouri, a town of about 100,000 people, where much of my research was conducted, there was no local for-profit recycling company; however, the one in St. Louis dispatches trucks to the Goodwill and Salvation Army in Columbia (over 100 miles away) to pick up their surplus.

Many municipalities do not offer any—let alone convenient—textile recycling. This is their loss because it often proves lucrative and can subsidize the rest of a recycling program. However, textiles do not easily fit into an established curbside recycling program because natural fibers mold and mildew when wet. The typical solution to this problem requires setting up big waterproof boxes where donors can drop their items.

I have recently supervised an independent study project where students were charged with setting up a small recycling facility in Boonville, Missouri, a small rural town about twenty minutes from Columbia. The company, called Unlimited Opportunities, is a center for training physically and mentally challenged adults. Employees used to paint parts for a major heavy machinery maker. When that company sent their operations overseas, it left the unemployed workers and a giant warehouse, complete with docks and a baling machine, empty. When I looked at the space, I determined that it had fabulous potential as a recycling center that could be attached to a Goodwill-type charity shop. Boonville had none at the time. Expecting to get two or three fashion-merchandising students interested in helping set up the business in exchange for independent study credit, I put a call out—and got twelve students to sign on!

They put together a business plan, pitched it to Unlimited Opportunities' board of directors and within six weeks, the shop opened. In the interim, the students had trained workers to sort clothing and polish shoes. Excess clothes are baled and sold to for-profit recyclers and today, Savvy Seconds has grown to a recycling house that not only sells used clothing but that also recycles aluminum, plastics and cardboard—a much-needed resource for the rural community. It's an economic, environmental, and human success story.

Americans discard huge volumes, but also huge value. Today, with resources and landfill space becoming ever more dear, it is a value that we can't afford to waste.

Using What Others Toss Out

Harry Matusow, President, Jimtex Yarns

Stefanie Zeldin, Corporate Marketing and Brand Manager, ECO2cottonTM

Jimtex Yarns
325 Chestnut Street, Suite 725
Philadelphia, PA 19106
szeldin@martexfiber.com
(703) 255-1678
www.jimtexyarns.com
www.eco2cotton.com
www.martexfiber.com

To make a t-shirt, virgin cotton yarn is typically knit into a tube. Then, a machine cuts away shapes to free the sleeves and neckline. The body of the shirt continues to be constructed while the cuttings, which can amount to 40 percent of the total fabric, fall to the floor. The cuttings are swept up, thrown into bags and many times, especially in emerging economies, landfilled or incinerated. All that waste is even more shameful when you consider the environmental costs associated with creating cotton fabric. The World Wildlife Fund reports that 25 percent of all insecticides are used each year on cotton fields around the world.

Recycling textiles allows potential waste to become product, and ensures every bit of value is squeezed out of our resources. It also meets a demand for cotton that does not necessarily have to be virgin (and all of the chemicals, energy, land and water that the process entails). Recycled cotton offers numerous environmental advantages. It directs waste away from landfills and incinerators. It does not require the extensive use of natural resources such as water and land that even organic cotton requires. It does not need to be soaked in synthetic dyes. The colors generated are based on the colors of the waste clippings.

Jimtex's ECO2cottonTM recycled cotton yarn, suitable for apparel knits and wovens as well as decorative home items, looks good, feels good and comes in a wide range of colors. It also presents an available, immediately viable yarn choice for companies that wish to support environmentally responsible textile manufacturing. Approximately 5,000 bales (3.2 million pounds) of organic cotton were grown in the U.S. last year. This year Jimtex will spin twice that amount of pre-consumer textile waste into ECO2cottonTM yarn. Clearly, ECO2cottonTM yarn represents an important step toward making fashion a closed-loop industry.

To develop this eco-smart product, Jimtex developed innovative proprietary technology and relied on the extensive expertise and operations of its parent company, Martex Fiber Southern Corporation.

Although Martex Fiber still operates at its original location, most of its textile waste collection has moved offshore, following the migration of mills to countries with lower labor costs. Martex Fiber has established strategic business partnerships with facilities in Honduras and El Salvador that collect cotton waste from the mills of some of the most popular t-shirt and underwear brands in the U.S.

It is vital to coach mills on how to recoup maximum profit from what they had previously thrown away. For example, a mill can expect to receive a much better price simply by separating its red cotton clippings from the blue ones. Similarly, it saves money by compacting its fiber on site, using a baling press. Compacted fiber is less expensive to ship than fiber that is merely thrown into bags. Martex Fiber also guides factories as to which items have high and low value. It advises when it makes economic sense to spend time carefully sorting.

After acquiring the regenerated cotton from Martex Fiber, Jimtex blends color, fiber content and yarn quality to spin the fibers into new yarn. A small percentage of a synthetic material, such as acrylic or polyester, is added during spinning. This acts as glue. At present, Jimtex uses virgin acrylic from Mexico, Europe or Turkey; however, it has recently located a post-consumer recycled polyester company in the U.S. and plans on using this polyester to produce a 100 percent recycled yarn.

Jimtex is also distinguished by advancements in color-blending technique. Every day, Jimtex must create standardized shades of yarn from an ever-changing array of source material. To meet this challenge, it employs a process comparable to mixing paint. A navy blue from t-shirt stock, a bright blue from underwear and black from socks may blend to create beautiful heather. Each color is developed as a formula that can later be mimicked.

By blending dyes, one can achieve an almost limitless range of colors. Potential clients are given a menu of 70 color options, with recipes, raw materials and perhaps even finished yarn. Ultimately, customers are satisfied because the yarn is environmentally responsible, comes in beautiful, unique color blends, and costs less than conventional yarn.

Jimtex is also trying to lessen its energy consumption. By obtaining waste from local manufacturers, recycling such materials into new yarn, and then supplying the original manufacturer with new, recycled yarn, the company is able to support the local economy, shorten shipping distances and minimize waste.

The ECO2cotton™ brand and Web site create awareness about the environmental advantages of recycled materials and allow Jimtex to target the high-end t-shirt and knit market. They are also participating in programs to make socks, sweaters, t-shirts, hats, fleece, uniforms, and hand-knitting yarns and blankets, among many other woven items. So far, the response to ECO2cotton™ has been tremendous.

OLD SOLUTIONS TO
NEW CHALLENGES

A 5,000-Year-Old Fiber Gets a Fashion Update

Dr. James M. Vreeland, Jr., Anthropologist and Business Founder
Peru Naturtex Partners

www.perunaturtex.com

Anthropologically speaking, the concept of sustainable fashion was only possible when fashion became unsustainable—that is, when people began outliving their wardrobes, probably sometime after the Industrial Revolution of the 18th century. Before then, clothing, scarce and dear, was taken to the grave by commoners and nobles alike. Not even the appetites of legendary garmen terrorists like Marie Antoinette or the 15th century Inca King Atahualpa (immortalized by one Spanish chronicler for discarding his royal tunics once stained) were voracious enough to deplete fiber stocks or sully streams. But the invention of the cotton gin, spinning jenny and Jacquard loom allowed cotton fiber to be available not only worldwide but also year-round, and at remarkably low prices. Low prices encourage overindulgence, wasteful distribution and commercially uncontrollable consumerism.

Conventional cotton cultivation is blighted. In the U.S., cotton is subsidized to such a degree that, were these artificial and Byzantinely complex price-support schemes removed, cotton cultivation would no doubt disappear altogether. Inversely, if impoverished cotton farmers in Francophone Africa and parts of Southern Asia and Latin America were paid the "real" price for their "white gold," the emerging economies of those areas would boom. Data from the Pesticide Action Network UK fingers cotton farming as the single largest user of chemical inputs, contaminating factories, fields and the families struggling to survive on them.

Paradoxically, despite cotton's chemical dependency and reputation as a despoiler of green farming acres and peasant economies around the globe, no consolidated demand for organic cotton clothing or sustainable fashion exists anywhere—except perhaps on these pages and on the Internet. The truth is that the investment in "eco-fashion" is driven almost entirely by brands and their owners, by designers and dogooders, but rarely by consumers. Happily, their vision is starting to pay off!

Let's look at one case, the revival of naturally pigmented and organically cultivated cotton in Peru. The first Native Americans Christopher Columbus and his ragtag crew saw were well-dressed in handmade cotton clothing. Undoubtedly this cotton clothing was striped with naturally pigmented yarns spun from hand-picked, organically cultivated fiber nearly double in staple length of any variety then known in the Old World. In a subsequent voyage, "Indians" presented Columbus, son of a weaver himself, with a ball of yarn from a storehouse stocked with some 12,000 pounds of it on the island of Cuba.

In 1971, as a volunteer in the National Museum of Anthropology in Lima, Peru, I shared a small conservation laboratory with a resident population of fleas, rats, a snake and a monkey. My task was to examine pre-Columbian textiles, trying to figure out how best to preserve them. However, what I would see through the Bausch & Lomb stereoscopic microscope would set me off on another trail altogether. What caught my eye were some intriguing dark masses inside the cotton fibers' walls that imparted color to the fabric. They did not appear to be the result of dye, so I began to ask around at universities in Lima: was it possible that some cotton was naturally pigmented? The answer, often derisively given, was categorically no. Cotton was, and is, only white! The pigmentation, the experts insisted, must be the result of oxidation or of some age-related degradation process. Dr. Victor Antonio Rodriguez Suy, a professor of anthropology at the National University of Trujillo and a descendant of the Mochic ethnic group, told me otherwise. To prove that colored cotton did exist, he drove me out to an abandoned strip of beach, where he pointed out some scrubby cotton plants growing in sunken, sandy fields of obviously prehistoric origin. These cotton plants bore reddish-brown fibers unlike anything recorded in my text-books. Entranced, I traveled the area searching for plants and textiles with naturally-pigmented fibers. I found shades of off-white, ecru, brown, chocolate and even mauve. It was challenging work, because the descendants of the Mochic Indians of the north coast guarded their plants closely.

Months turned into 20 years of seeking all the information I could find in museums, libraries and in the field, at ancient sites, and by talking with everyone I met about naturally-colored cotton. Ancestors of the Mochic people cultivated cotton in a myriad of hues 5,000 years ago. These present-day descendants quietly maintain some of these cultivars, and have taught me the most about naturally-colored cotton.

With concrete evidence that colored cotton grew in the Andes, I began looking for similar evidence on other continents. The story was always the same. Over the centuries, the traditional or ancient landraces of colored cotton were bred into predominantly creamy white strains. Following the advent of the cotton gin and inexpensive industrial dyes, white cotton reigned supreme. Dyeing white cotton yielded a wide color palette cheaply and quickly. Moreover, unlike naturally pigmented cottons, no specialized harvest techniques were needed to laboriously separate by hand different colors and fiber characteristics. By the end of the last century, white cotton almost completely replaced the indigenous, colored cotton cultivars grown in Africa, Asia, Central and South America. Colored plants survived only in seed banks kept by some agricultural departments around the world and in small, traditional communities. These pigmented cottons have undergone a revival recently. Few people know that virtually all the colored cotton plants used commercially in the West come from pre-Columbian stocks created by the indigenous peoples of South America.

Modern Egyptian cotton, for example, is derived from a South American progenitor (most probably G. barbadense). Slavers apparently brought this cotton to northern Africa from the New World. First described in 1820 or so, this strain originally produced a long, strong lint with a golden-brown color. It was interbred with local plants to yield new commercial selections: ashmouni, a brown stock; mitafifi, which was darker brown with a longer lint and gave rise to American-Egyptian yuma cotton in 1908; and, finally, what is now called pima cotton. Pima is the name of a Native American tribe, members of which helped to experimentally grow an extra-long staple variety of G.babadense. Developed in Arizona, it was obtained from an Egyptian form—originally from Peru— and cultivated there during the past century.

Colored cotton plants from the eastern Mediterranean region and Asia apparently reached the U.S. during the colonial period. Cultivars of G. arboreum arrived, as did those of G. hirsutum and G. barbadense. Colored cotton was hand-woven and spun, and even machine-woven at times, in several Southern states. In the heart of the Mississippi Delta, for example, golden-brown cotton has been grown for more than two centuries by a small group of Acadian spinners. Despite scattered pockets of colored cotton cultivation, however, it never took off commercially in the U.S. Yet in the 1990s, naturally colored cotton made a sudden but short-lived reappearance as a fashion item. Big U.S. clothing manufacturers such as Patagonia, Levi Strauss and Esprit, not to mention several European companies, began to buy organic cotton, environmentally-friendly fibers grown with the absence of synthetic chemicals or genetically modified organisms. Sadly, consumers quickly lost interest. However, with concerns about endocrine disrupters and rising cancer rates, the organic cotton movement has regained momentum. Currently, some 200,000 acres in the U.S. and a dozen other countries produce organic cotton, including naturally pigmented cottons that do not have to be dyed.

Chemical compounds from conventionally grown cotton not only harm the workers who use them but also leach into the soil, reaching groundwater, rivers and streams, killing fish and contaminating livestock. Moreover, once it has been harvested, white cotton is usually bleached, which involves chlorine-based processes that produce dioxins. The cotton is then dyed with a host of other chemicals, many of which include heavy metals that often end up in the water stream. Interestingly, these chemicals were also used as weapons in the quasi-ethnically, quasi-economically motivated strike against colored cotton carried out during most of the 20th century by the Peruvian government.

Indeed, when I created the Native Cotton Project in 1982, I discovered that its mission, to revive the cultivation and use of colored cotton, required the governmental reversal of a century-long policy. Fortunately, we had the support of the Peruvian ministries of labor and tourism. Beginning in 1931, the Peruvian government issued a series of laws and decrees aimed at destroying perennial, pigmented forms of native cotton in an effort to protect the all-white varieties that were commercially viable. On the pretext of eradicating cotton pests, the elimination of all the possible alternative plant hosts—including landraces of colored cotton, the Peruvian kapok tree (Bombax discolor) and even a lintless cotton (G. raimondii)—were decreed. Furthermore, pesticides were liberally applied (even though the boll weevil does not thrive in Peru), and the long-standing, successful tradition of crop rotation was abandoned.

Although the pest-control program, cloned from USDA models, proved to be an expensive and misbegotten failure, it was still adhered to in the 1980s, with devastating consequences. Much of the genetic variation present earlier in the century had been irreversibly eroded, abandoned by indigenous farmers or suppressed by a legion of new plant pathogens that arose after the massive pesticide application. Even the survival of the commercial all-white cotton was severely threatened. In 1990 a Peruvian "environmental code" finally made the eradication practice illegal; nevertheless, pesticides remain pervasive. At present, the annual consumption of pesticides in Peru reached an all-time high: about 18 pounds (eight kilograms) of pesticides per person per year. Experts say that only one percent of the insect pest damage is being controlled now.

Nonetheless, over the past decade or so, we have been able to rebuild the stock of naturally colored cotton using traditional, organic methods of production. On many of our farms, large pests are removed by hand (children often drown them in a water-filled jar) and insect-repellent plants are grown among the crop rows. These techniques are pre-Colombian in origin. Archaeological sites from A.D. 1250 show that cotton was grown in rotation with squash. Ancient soil samples also reveal the presence of pollen grains from a weedy shrub, Lippia, dismissed by most farmers as useless. Years of questioning indigenous farmers turned up one octogenarian who identified the plant as mastrante. He grew it in a row next to his native cotton plants to control a pest called the cotton stainer (Dysdercus peruvianus), which ruins cotton by puncturing the seeds and releasing oils that stain the fiber. The old farmer did this by periodically cutting down several mastrante plants, drying them in the sun and, when the wind was right, igniting them. Pungent smoke from the desiccated shrubs wafted through the cotton fields, driving out the bugs.

Today the Native Cotton Project maintains 75 landraces of white and naturally pigmented cottons, despite the often hostile attitude of the government. Some 15,000 peasants and indigenous farmers who grow these cottons in dozens of plots throughout Peru are by far the largest single group of naturally colored lint producers worldwide. Ironically, and perhaps fittingly, the Minister of Agriculture himself cultivates naturally pigmented cotton as a hobby in his hometown in northern Peru.

The Native Cotton Project grew steadily, and in 1993, a textile company in Arequipa approached us to market naturally colored cotton products internationally. We chose Pakucho ("brown cotton" in the ancient Inca language) as our brand name. In 1997 Peru Naturtex Partners was founded as a contract manufacturing company and now produces more than 125 different colored cotton yarns, textiles and apparel. SKAL Int., a Dutch inspection organization, certifies all our cotton fiber and fabrics as organic. In 2005, Naturtex became the first textile company in the Americas also to be certified as Fair Trade by the prestigious FLO CERT organization of Europe.

Our colored cotton is not only organic and fairly traded, as a lucrative cash crop, it represents an alternative to clandestine coca leaf production for cocaine. Since the Native Cotton Project began in 1982, we estimate that over 3,000 hectares have been converted to organic fiber, replacing the illegally cultivated coca leaf. This "Drug Free" initiative bears fruit not only in the fields, but also among families that can now reunite after decades of a precarious existence in a marginal and hostile jungle world. After we founded the Native Cotton Project, many similar revival efforts have sprouted up throughout the Americas. In the hills of Santander in Colombia, for instance, a small group of student-led peasant producers has brought back native cotton spinning and weaving as a rural development project. In the highlands of Guatemala, the Ixchel Museum of Guatemala City is leading a revival project in communities where brown cotton, or ixcoco, was traditionally spun until the practice almost died out. In the Bolivian Oriente, the Chiquitano Indians hope to revive organic cotton cultivation. Perhaps most significantly, in the north desert coast of Peru, the Morrope Indian project to revive colored cotton cultivation and craft production has been awarded several donations from UNESCO and the Gilles Foundation in Brussels. A low-interest loan from the Ecologic Finance group in Cambridge, Massachusetts, promotes the cultivation of native and extra-long staple varieties of native white cotton among the peasant farmers of the region.

The future of colored cotton looks bright in many places. It has gained prominence in the U.S. and Europe. This year, Peru's naturally pigmented and organically grown cotton exports will exceed $100 million, making it the world's greatest exporter of naturally colored cotton. It's a fitting tribute to the many thousands of native Andeans who created, developed, and eventually shared with the world the luxuriously long pima and earth-colored cotton fiber we know and enjoy today.

Cleaner Cotton Grown in Color

Sally Fox, Organic Cotton Breeder and Mom
Vreseis Limited

PO Box 69
Guinda, CA 95637
www.vreseis.com

I am a scientist and a businesswoman, who just happens to have been able to combine my awe of the environment, biology, and textiles to produce Foxfibre®, the first naturally colored cotton that could be spun on modern machines. It has been a life-long commitment, fascinating and deeply satisfying, though also frustrating at times.

My passion for my work was fired by experiences early in my life that made me profoundly distrust conventional farming and textile manufacturing practices that rely heavily on the use of manmade chemicals. In 1971, as a high school student, a wonderful new teacher changed my life. Miss Wangari, a Stanford Ph.D. candidate from Kenya, taught a short course on entomology. Her stories of Africa and pesticide disasters filled me with wonder and horror. I felt, immediately and deeply, that I had found my calling. She arranged for me to intern at a brand new Palo Alto-based company called Zoecon Corporation, which developed the use of insect-specific hormones to manage other insect pest populations in an environmentally sound way.

In college, I taught hand-spinning, my hobby since age twelve. One of my good friends from our spinning guild had a daughter who was a high school textile arts instructor. Recently, she had become a convalescent, rendered essentially brain-dead by exposure to dyestuffs while teaching. I had never thought about dyes as poisonous, but her story made a deep impression on me. I soon found that the same companies that made pesticides also made dyes for textiles, and I became determined to avoid both products of the chemical industry. In my own spinning, knitting and weaving, I used only natural fiber colors, of which there are a surprising number.

A few years later, while working as an integrated pest management specialist for an independent plant breeder, I found what appeared to be the panacea for the ills associated with cotton cultivation and textile manufacture. It was tucked in a little paper bag at the back of a greenhouse drawer: a raw brown cotton boll with the seeds attached to the lint. The plant breeder let me know that they had originally been obtained in hopes of introducing their disease resistance to susceptible white cotton strains, but the project had been dropped. It was thought that separating the desirable disease resistance from the undesirable color would be too difficult. I loved the color and thought we could market naturally colored and naturally disease- and pest-free cotton. My boss laughed and suggested that I pursue this on my own time, which I did and still do. I now know why he smiled so broadly; this was no small task to take on.

Though the boll that I found in that drawer was new to me, naturally colored cotton had been grown in the United States for centuries. In the antebellum South, slaves could only grow colorful cotton. It was a crop with which they could clothe themselves but receive no money. (Money, of course, was something they legally could not possess.) I suspect that it was enslaved farmers who developed the first green cotton. The only record of it comes from the southeastern United States. After the Civil War, the tradition of growing brown and green cotton persisted through the Cajun people.

First in a greenhouse and later on a couple of rented acres, I carried out my passion for selecting for the most attractive and commercially viable strains of brown and green cotton. At first, I looked for two qualities: color consistency and fiber length. Fiber length determines how easy it is to spin: the longer the fiber, the easier. Mechanized spinners require very long fibers, which white cotton is bred for. (Before he developed spinning machinery, Sir Richard Arkwright earned his living as a wigmaker and was one of the first to dye the hair in his wigs. That the inventor of cotton machinery was first an accomplished dyer may explain why all the machinery was designed for the fiber qualities of white cotton, which can be dyed any color one wishes.)

Brown fibers tend to be short. At first I assessed their "spin-ability" myself. Then, concerned that I might be learning to spin short fibers rather than letting the fibers grow longer, I began sending samples to hand-spinning guilds around the nation. These master hand-spinners made an extraordinary discovery: boiling cotton yarn sets its twist. They found that some of my samples lost their pigment while others actually became more intensely colored. (In a subsequent experiment, I laundered the latter kind of cotton repeatedly, and found that the color kept deepening over the course of 50 washes.) From that point on, I selected for color-fastness as well. Indeed, when I applied for my first plant protection certificate, I was told that the examiner was really impressed by my strain's lasting color.

It wasn't until I received some surprise funding and had the chance to take my samples down to the fiber lab at Texas Tech University that I learned more about what made my cotton distinctive. Any given cotton fiber, as you may know, is just one very, very long cell. If you slice one cross-wise and peer at it through a microscope, you will see rings, like tree rings, and a hole in the middle, called the lumen. The rings come from daily deposited layers of cellulose. Between these is a waxy substance. In the brown cotton, tannins (a large group of chemicals that also makes coffee brown and wine red) constituted the pigment. In the colorfast varieties, the tannins reside mainly in the lumen, although also on the outer layer of the fiber. Boiling the fibers drew the tannins outward toward the edge of the shaft. The pigment for the green fibers was already located near the surface, in the interstitial wax. As you would expect, all the green cotton retained its color.

It was at the same lab that I learned that my brown cotton had fibers long enough to spin using machines. I finally had a commercial product.

I tended my 40-acre plot of mostly experimental plants in the San Joaquin Valley, California's center of cotton production. To the surrounding farmers, I was an eccentric outsider: a woman entomologist breeding naturally grown cotton under organic conditions—and a San Francisco Bay-area native, no less! To them, I was the agricultural equivalent of Nancy Pelosi. Their tolerance turned to malice when I started getting business. Japanese mills vied for my green crop, especially. Suddenly, my neighbors began to worry that my crop could contaminate theirs. Perhaps the ideal of uniformity became engrained in the minds of cotton farmers from the days when the law, in an effort to establish commodification, only permitted one strand of cotton. Cotton, however, is a self-pollinating plant and risk of cross-pollination is very low.

I heard the grumbling, but business had never been better. Levi's was thrilled with the jeans they wove out of the brown; Land's End designed a striped sweater out of my brown and green yarns, and Fieldcrest Cannon had incorporated brown cotton into their sheets and reported that their customers were thrilled by their improved texture and color. Then one day I received a phone call from the owner of the company that delinted my cotton seed. He begged me to have my cotton delinted in the middle of the season. Otherwise, he said, he'd have to lay off his crew because everyone else's harvest was so delayed. I was disconcerted. For years, I had delinted my cotton after all the other farmers. Then I'd paid for the machines to be cleaned before next year's harvest. At this stage, crop contamination was a real possibility, because seeds could get stuck in the machines. When the caller assured me that a state authority would oversee the process, I foolishly consented. Sure enough, the farmer who delinted after me found ten brown cotton plants in his fields the next year. Though I paid for the plants to be removed, the State of California's Department of Agriculture passed a resolution that outlawed any growing or breeding of naturally colored cotton. My choices were to stop production or move. I moved.

Within a year, the mill that was spinning the yarns for my customers received a strong message from Cotton Incorporated that spinning anything but white cotton was "un-American." I heard about this from the vice president of the mill who called me in an uproar, having just resigned under pressure. With yarn production stopped, my orders were cancelled, gravely compromising my client relationships. By the end of the

'90s, I closed my company. I kept my seeds and my oldest customers, however, and continue to grow brown and green cotton. For the time being, while I am raising my daughter, I am satisfied with that.

I feel that the cotton industry has encouraged the perception that naturally colored cotton is more of a nuisance than it is worth. They claim that the natural colors are limiting rather than choice-broadening. However, my cotton offers many more advantages than simply the colors nature imbue it. Naturally colored cotton holds huge potential to make the dyeing process more efficient and effective. My fiber does not need to be dyed to be a beautiful hue, but it can be dyed and in fact could significantly improve the ecological profile of that process. Certainly, in terms of striving toward sustainability, the dye industry needs all the help it can get.

Color is a very expensive additive. Cotton, which is composed primarily of cellulose, is difficult to dye compared with the protein fibers such as wool and silk. When I was researching this in the '90s, I discovered that one pound of "low-impact"-dyed cotton uses 100 gallons of water and generates toxic waste that should be collected and stored in a toxic waste facility. Dyeing one pound of cotton costs 50 cents for the dyeing (including water, power and dye) and two dollars for the toxic waste cleanup. Of course, this latter expense only applies if environmental regulations require it. The '90s saw responsible mills put out of business as mills in parts of the world without regulations dumped—and still dump—vast quantities of toxic waste into waterways.

The phenomenon continues today on a global level. While mills in the U.S., Europe and Japan are spending two dollars per pound to clean up the dye waste, their competitors in India, China, Indonesia and elsewhere are allowed to export their goods into these countries without spending that money to clean up the waste.

The same problem occurs with cotton farming. U.S. farmers cannot use cheap DDT anymore. Yet much of the cotton in other countries is grown with this pesticide. At one mill I visited in India, they imported U.S. cotton to make products for Europe, where regulations prohibit importing DDT, and then used their own Indian cotton with DDT residue for export to the U.S. It is no surprise that DDT levels are rising in our estuaries and will continue to do so with every laundering of these cheaper textiles.

If our laws required any imported textile to be grown and processed by U.S. textile standards, we would see immediate improvement. First, we might save the last of our domestic mills, which are now barely keeping afloat. We would have a significant decrease worldwide in the release of toxins, such as DDT, into the environment. And mills around the globe would have a financial incentive to explore the use of natural colored fibers.

At present, the three dominant dye colors are black, khaki and indigo blue. Mixing brown and green cotton with white cotton in various proportions creates many different shades of khaki. Substantial savings could be made using brown cotton as a base for black dye. Dyeing white cotton black is a wasteful process. Though a great deal of black dye is used, inevitably, the items fade quickly. The lab at Texas Tech determined that brown cotton required far less dye than white cotton to achieve superior color-fastness. The scientists attributed this to the tannins in the fiber. Tannins are a mordant, meaning that they fix dyes. Because of their chemical properties, organically raised brown and green cotton do not require a substantial proportion of conventionally used chemicals, both during the fiber cultivation and dyeing stages.

Tannin lends naturally grown cotton other surprising virtues. Tannins give brown cottons significant natural flame resistance and are potent antioxidants. Our skin can absorb these therapeutic chemicals from a garment. Imagine wearing clothes that protect you from fire and sickness, preserve water purity, use relatively little energy and agricultural chemicals and did not threaten a rural family with pesticide drift!

We have come to depend on cotton for clothes, and that is probably a good thing. Among its environmental virtues are renewability and biodegradability. However, instead of clinging to the pest-prone, dye-thirsty cotton we know, we should take advantage of this plant's full genetic diversity to mitigate the environmental problems we have caused. It would be a shame if industry politics kept us from such a straightforward solution. As for me, I dream of being able to do my work with these marvelous plants again, both in the fields and in the mills.

A Fair Deal for Farmers

Damien Sanfilippo, Cotton Project Officer
Pesticide Action Network UK

Development House
56-64 Leonard Street
London EC2A 4LT
www.pan-uk.org

Cotton production is crucial to the economy of many developing countries. When West African nations gained their independence in the late 1950s, they saw cotton farming as an engine for economic development: white gold would earn them self-sufficiency. In India, cotton spinning and weaving became the symbol of the anti-colonial movement: Mahatma Gandhi wanted a cotton-spinning wheel in every house.

Half a century later, these would-be cotton fairy tales lack a happy ending. More cotton farmers live in India than any other country, but most of them barely cling to survival. Unable to pay back their debts to pesticide suppliers, hundreds have committed suicide in recent years. According to the Human

Development Index, such West African countries as Benin, Burkina Faso, Mali, Chad and Côte d'Ivoire, for which cotton accounts for the great majority of their export revenue, remain among the 15 poorest countries in the world.

In addition to failing to improve the economic security of these countries' citizens, conventional cotton production has a devastating impact on their environment, and on the health of farmers and their communities. Chemical-intensive cotton production damages biodiversity, contaminates soil and water resources, and depletes soil fertility and structure. More hazardous pesticides are sprayed on cotton than on any other crop. The damage goes well beyond the cotton fields. Researchers at James Cook University in Australia recently exposed a potential catastrophe-in-the-making. Pesticides used on Australian cotton farms may be contributing to the progressive destruction of one of our planet's most magnificent ecological treasures, the Great Barrier Reef. Evidence is also slowly emerging that pesticide contamination of water might explain why amphibians in particular are mysteriously disappearing worldwide.

But corals and amphibians are not the only species affected. The full and exact extent of acute pesticide poisonings among cotton farmers and their families is unknown, as it is rarely monitored nationally, and has never been monitored globally. However, a Pesticide Action Network survey documented 67 deaths in only two districts of Benin during the 2001 cotton growing season. At this rate, the global figure for cotton farmers in developing countries would total 16,100 annual deaths. It is reasonable to suspect that this figure is actually low. Among those who die or are made ill from pesticide poisoning, few make it to a hospital, and fewer are correctly diagnosed. Even less is known on the extent of the damage caused by the chronic effects of pesticide exposure, although many of the relevant chemicals have been linked to infertility and cancer.

Surprisingly, the social, environmental and health effects of conventional cotton production have only been addressed recently. The most broadly effective response to these problems is organic cotton. From its humble and recent beginnings on some Turkish and American cotton farms less than 20 years ago, organic cotton has rapidly spread all over the world and to the mass market. There is no major newspaper or magazine in Europe or America that has not covered a story about organic cotton. But what the media fails to report is how wide-ranging the benefits of organic cotton are. Organic cotton is not only gentler on the environment, it challenges the mechanisms of the oldest and most unethical of global industries, the textile industry. In doing so, it also offers a novel trade model.

It is important to understand how the textile industry managed to get away, until very recently, with unethical trading and environmental practices. Textile supply chains are extremely long, complex and opaque to the point that consumers, located at one end of the chain, can be completely ignorant of its beginning: fiber production and the cotton farmers. A few years ago, when consumers first peeked down the supply chain, they discovered sweatshops. With the public gaze upon them, retailers in the West tried to take responsibility: not an easy task, as most major clothing retailers have well over 2,000 suppliers. Fiber production is still much further down the supply chain than cut-and-sew operations, and the nature of the industry makes it nearly impossible to trace the origin of the fiber.

Several months ago, campaigners from the U.K.-based Environmental Justice Foundation uncovered the horrendous conditions in which cotton is produced in Uzbekistan, the world's third largest exporter. In a well-documented report, they revealed the environmental ruin and quasi-enslavement of a whole nation for the benefit of a small ruling class. Shocked, some retail executives tried to figure out whether, indeed, there was Uzbek cotton at the beginning of their supply chain. Try as they did, many simply couldn't determine the truth. Spinning mills buy from cotton traders dealing in cotton from all over the world. They blend the fibers irrespective of origin. When the yarn leaves the factory, it is no longer traceable to one point of origin.

This lack of traceability makes it all too convenient for retailers to turn a blind eye to the conditions surrounding fiber production. In the case of the clothing industry, corporate social and environmental responsibility does not yet apply to the misfortune of small-scale cotton farmers. Fifty million cotton farmers are an integral part of this textile industry; yet they are anonymous, invisible.

The highly segmented system also keeps farmers' prices down. Clothing retailers shop around for the cheapest manufacturers, who shop around for the cheapest fabric, and so on. Cotton farmers, at the end of the chain, are squeezed to the maximum. The actual cost of cotton fibers in a garment sold on the high street is typically less than two percent of the retail price. In order to increase their yields and thus their profit, many farmers are tempted to step on the pesticide treadmill. However, as pests develop resistance to pesticides, farmers' income plummets. The unfair competition created by subsidies to American and European farmers drives the price further down. This cycle keeps cotton farmers in developing countries in a perpetual state of poverty and indebtedness — good news for the agrochemical companies, which make $2.2 billion selling cotton pesticides each year.

How can organic cotton break this cycle? Organic cotton is grown without the use of chemical pesticides, synthetic fertilizers and genetically-modified (GM) seeds. Organic farmers aim to restore a natural balance within the farm by emphasizing healthy and well-structured soils. In such an environment, pests are not systematically destroyed. With careful management and an understanding of the role of

predators, friendly bugs and good agricultural practices, such as crop rotation, farmers can contain pest
damage and enhance yields. Biodiversity and wildlife
are preserved. The benefits of organic cotton to the
environment and to the health of farmers and their
families are instantly recognizable and have been
documented elsewhere. Its benefits are wide-ranging, too: organic cotton allows farmers to engage in a
much more equitable trade.

Organic cotton offers farmers direct financial benefits. Farmers have a better income through the combined effect of premium price and lower production
costs, because they haven't had to buy chemicals.
Savings on health care are an added financial bonus.
Crop rotation, an underlying principle of organic
agriculture, allows farmers to diversify their source of
income, thus mitigating the risk associated with cotton's highly variable market price (while contributing
to community food security). Cotton farmers in
Benin were recently asked to indicate their prime
reasons for going organic. The survey revealed that,
although farmers appreciated increased income, better health, and environmental benefits, a surprising
motivation topped their list: the organic cotton supply chain pays them on time, usually soon after the
cotton is collected from the village. Conventional
farmers typically wait for months—sometimes a
whole year—before they get paid, thus worsening
their debt problems. Although many modern-day
suppliers in all sectors, faced with the all-powerful

purchasing power of supermarkets and giant retail chains, have resigned themselves to waiting 90 days before payment, none would accept such a considerable delay—none could survive it.

As a consequence, organic cotton offers farming households more financial stability. But it also offers a more equitable division of the family income between husbands and wives. While women are often discouraged—sometimes banned—from conventional cotton farming, they usually enthusiastically engage in organic cotton production, as it does not mean exposure to chemicals and the associated high rates of miscarriage.

It can even be claimed that organic cotton has changed the nature of the whole supply chain. In order to produce a t-shirt labeled 100 percent organic cotton, the organic fiber needs to remain completely separate from any conventional cotton fiber and, as a consequence, cannot enter the conventional supply chain. In the 1990s, organic cotton pioneers had no choice but to build their own supply chains from scratch. In doing so, they invented a whole new model of textile supply chain based on the revolutionary (for the textile industry) concept of partnership.

In the vertically integrated supply chains, farmers became business partners, on par with spinners, weavers, manufacturers, retailers, etc. Every partner plays a part in ensuring the success of the business model. In return, contributions and fair returns are shared among all partners. In this system, all partners have a voice and discuss each one's needs, requirements and aspirations. In sharp contrast to the conventional system, farmers are celebrated. Retailers commit to buying the farmers' harvest at a reasonable price and may assist farmers through pre-financing. For their part, farmers commit to providing retailers with a supply of quality, organically-certified cotton. In this way, smaller retailers have been able to secure their supply, despite the recent fiber shortage caused by large companies entering the market. Lastly, through the correspondence between the organic field certification and the final label on the garment, a link is established between the farmer and the consumer: the chain is finally closed. Consumers can see the face of the farmer in the cotton they buy and wear.

Another advantage to undertaking a partnership is being able to share risk. Risks are immense throughout the textile industry, but they are especially great at the fiber production stage. Agriculture always implies uncontrollable vicissitudes. Cotton especially is notoriously subject to pest infestation and weather, which affect both yield and quality. Small-scale farming amplifies these factors. In comparison, the cotton spinning mill is protected by spreading its risk over a variety of suppliers from different regions.

A farmer of rainfed organic cotton produces his or her crop in the most sustainable manner; but these farmers are also the most vulnerable. No financial or legislative "nets" are in place to break their fall. In effect, they are penalized for sustainable production. If we, as a society, consider rewarding companies that reduce energy consumption and greenhouse gas emissions, we should likewise assist farmers who are making an even deeper commitment to sustainable practice with much more at stake.

Instead of support, farmers get outrageously high interest rates. Most banks are not enthusiastic about giving microcredit loans to farmers even at the best of times. Since banks view the use of pesticides as a form of security, they are slow to loan to organic cotton farmers. And because there is no assurance that it will rain, they are especially reluctant to loan to rain-fed organic farmers. Only by charging extremely high interest rates do they feel they can justify making such high-risk investments. These are rates that the farmers are expected to bear for at least six months while they wait for their crop to grow and for their clients to pay them. Most of these farmers are already extremely poor, yet they have no choice but to shoulder most of the risk associated with producing a cotton garment, of which they only receive a tiny fraction of the profit. The most important thing that a retailer can do to support sustainably cultivated cotton and the farmers whose lives are tied to it is to arrange for input advances on the harvest. Pre-financing is at the heart of realizing a fair trading model. This, and investing in infrastructure, is what pioneering organic cotton companies have done.

Organic cotton suggests a new model of efficient humanitarian aid through trade. Both humanitarian development aid and growing cotton were introduced to Africa with good intentions, but both often do more harm than good. Many observers argue that, over the last 50 years, most foreign development aid in Africa has enriched the powerful at the cost of ordinary people. In contrast, organic cotton projects empower farmers by offering them the training they need to farm their land in a sustainable, safe and economical way. The farmers understand how it improves their livelihood. African organic cotton farmers prefer to continue working hard and developing their own pest management methods rather than to pay for the expensive and often inappropriate technologies from abroad (e.g., chemicals or GM seeds) marketed as work-reducing miracle products. Organic cotton is a market-oriented approach: farmers see the rising demand from the EU and U.S. for sustainable and ethical goods, and respond to the opportunity of premium market access.

When consumers purchase African organic cotton products, they directly benefit the farmers. The money goes directly to help Africans realize their own goals for their lives, communities, and ultimately nations. Foreign aid, on the other hand, is sometimes burdened with an ulterior motive: introducing or maintaining the donor country's political influence in the region. The USAID's stated strategy with respect to cotton in West Africa is to "help" these countries adopt biotech technologies: GM seeds sold by U.S.-based companies. Despite its de facto inefficiencies, the French help maintain the cotton filiere they had set up in their colonies in the 1950s. Pouring money into this system prevents its collapse, but also preserves French influence. In addition, it means that less development aid is spent exploring a genuinely viable alternative, such as GM-free sustainable agriculture, either organic, or raised according to the principles of Integrated Crop Management. In the long run, replacing aid with trade is the most efficient way to reduce the economic differences between North and South. In our increasingly globalized world, so much of the world's peaceful future depends on our ability and willingness to lessen these inequalities.

The organic cotton sector is now facing its greatest challenge as it enters the mass market. Huge orders placed by Nike and Wal-Mart provide great opportunities to increase the sector and benefit farmers. However, they could also overwhelm the fledgling industry with their own agenda, upsetting the balance that organic farmers have so recently managed to strike. Will the giant players continue to use the ethical and equitable trading practices set up by the organic cotton pioneers, thus keeping organic cotton "fair"? Or will they try to replicate unfair practices? Crucially, will they uphold the pre-finance support? I feel that it is very unlikely that major retailers will do this. They premise their existence on the power they get from their size, and the ability to pay late gives them a crucial advantage. To do otherwise would go completely against their natural trading practices.

We—civil society, organic cotton farmers, and organic cotton pioneers—are watching the entry of organic cotton into the mass market with fear and anxiety, but also with hope. After all, it was we who lobbied the giant retailers, demonstrating how unethical their cotton was while praising organic cotton as the best alternative. We set in motion what has become a global battle for "green" credentials with respect to cotton.

This battle has mostly escaped our control, but we can offer some last, crucial pieces of guidance. In a nutshell, these companies who are so used to dictating the business agenda need to really listen to the farmers. They need to demonstrate that they actually understand the principles of the organic agriculture model, not just the opportunistic marketing it brings them. They need to promote organic agriculture on the fields, not only the labels on the shelves of their outlets. This requires just three small contributions:

- Retailers need to offer firm commitments to cotton farmers to buy part of their upcoming harvest at a fair price. This will facilitate access to credits and give financial institutions with the insurance they need to grant inexpensive loans to farmers. It is difficult for large retailers to commit to purchasing the totality of the future harvest because the risk of crop failure is too great. However, a commitment to buy 60 percent of the future harvest would give farmers security. Anything below 30 percent would not.

- Retailers also need to bring along their own banks. While "ethical banks" are on the rise, major conventional banks also need to give credit to small farmers from the developing word. Giant retailers have the power to educate their banks.

- Part of understanding the organic agriculture model is to see the fundamental principle of crop rotation and mixed cropping. Already, the demand for certified organic cotton is increasing much faster than the demand for the rotation crops. This presents a major threat to the organic system, as it pushes farmers to increase cotton production to the detriment of the rotation crops. Retailers, in effect, destroy the organic agriculture system, as well as threaten food security in the cotton-growing regions. Retailers need to buy the products of the organic farm as a "package," which include not only cotton, but the wide variety of rotation crops, which may include vegetables, groundnuts and shea nuts.

If giant retailers are willing to listen to farmers, they will find that they, too, can become ethical members of the organic cotton chain who participate in keeping fair trading practices at the heart of organic cotton. In this way, the "white gold" fairy tales may actually come true.

Dreaming of Organic Sheep

Matthew Mole, President and Founder
Vermont Organic Fiber Co.

52 Seymour Street, Suite 8
Middlebury, VT
www.vtorganicfiber.com

I grew up on a family farm in Vermont, where I firmly planted my roots in the sustainable agriculture industry. We did everything organically, because that's just how my family did things. We raised livestock, including sheep, but I did not enter the organic wool industry until years later, after having studied International Agricultural Economics at the University of Vermont. Following that I did several years of research on markets for Industrial Hemp as a possible agricultural crop for Vermont. The decision to work with organic wool was the result of my studies and research, and a timely conversation.

One day, a friend asked, "How about organic wool?" Inspired, I pursued the concept and eventually mustered some U.S. growers, establishing the framework for my company, the Vermont Organic Fiber Co. Since its founding in 2000, the company has grown while maintaining my original focus: to provide the highest quality yarns and fabrics made with certified organic wool. Over the years I've established a broad international network through which we source certified organic wool, develop products and processes, and establish strategic partnerships so that we can best meet the growing demands of companies looking to integrate organic fibers into their product lines. In the last year we have expanded the range of products which we offer through the introduction of blankets and hand knitting yarns sold under the O~Wool™ brand.

All yarns, fabrics, and finished products sold by the Vermont Organic Fiber Co. are sold under the O~Wool™ brand. All O~Wool™ yarns and fabrics are produced in accordance with the Organic Trade Association's (OTA) American Organic Standards Fiber: Post Harvest Handling, Processing, Record Keeping & Labeling.

As a member of the OTA Fiber Council steering committee from 1999 through 2006, I was actively involved in the development of these standards. This process, coupled with my own efforts to develop wool in a manner consistent with an organic philosophy, provided me with tremendous insight into the complexities and challenges of processing fiber organically. The entire process emphasized that we were involved in a very exciting movement. Not only were we supporting change in agricultural practices, we were also directly affecting positive change in an industry which has not always been particularly conscientious about the effects of its actions on the environment and communities in which it operates. Additionally, we were committed to develop the most globally comprehensive set of standards. It was a very exciting time and process, both for me and for the industry.

In order for one to sell an organic wool textile, the wool must originate from a certified organic farm. Organic livestock rules stipulate that sheep must receive organic feed and forage from the last third of their gestation, cannot receive synthetic hormones or have been genetically engineered, and cannot be exposed to synthetic pesticides (either internally or externally). These rules contrast with conventional practices in a number of ways. Organic sheep cannot be "dipped" in parasiticides, a common practice among larger wool producers, and farmers must not exceed the healthful carrying capacity of their grazing land.

The OTA Standards for Fiber cover all aspects of the handling and processing of organic textiles, from the point of leaving a farm through the final production of finished products. Whether it is specifying how materials are handled and segregated from non-organic fiber, eliminating the use of petrochemical-based agents in the production process, deciding what are allowable and prohibited dyestuffs, or ensuring that textile mills have appropriate waste treatment facilities, every aspect of textile processing was examined. I believe that one of the greatest accomplishments of this standard was the development of a comprehensive materials list and materials evaluation process. This provides the industry with clear guidelines on what materials are either allowed or prohibited in the processing of textiles, and the tools necessary to evaluate new materials as they are developed and introduced.

Conventional wool processing traditionally uses many products derived from petrochemical bases. Organic wool processors replace these with plant-based alternatives. For instance, during the wool scouring process (the first stage of processing where the lanolin and other impurities are washed out of the newly shorn wool) we use a vegetable-based soap. To lubricate fibers during spinning, we use coconut oil instead of a petroleum-derived product. It is actually a simpler treatment than the conventional, chemical one, but coconut oil is more expensive and not always readily available.

As one might expect, it has taken a few years' work to develop natural methods to replace the traditional ones without sacrificing quality. Fortunately, we are beginning with a great material. Wool is a complex natural fiber: it absorbs moisture yet repels water; it stretches, then springs back to shape; it resists dirt and repels odor yet absorbs dyes. Wool can absorb up to 30 percent of its weight in moisture, and wick it into the air. This keeps you warm when it's cool and cool when it's warm. Synthetics, by contrast, do not absorb moisture, but wick it away from the body to the fiber surface, which makes you feel clammy when it's warm and chilly when it's cool. The organic wool products that I am able to offer my customers now are as fine and soft as their conventional counterparts. Granted, some finishes like Superwash, a patented anti-felting process, will never meet organic standards. However, even in this area, I am confident that research will turn up organic techniques.

While demand for organic wool is increasing significantly in North America, currently most of the organic wool we process and sell comes from abroad. In part, this reflects the realities faced by the American sheep farmer, and flaws in the organic rule, which discourage transition to organic wool production systems. Greater availability of certified organic wool supplies is simply a result of the fact that most of the world's wool is produced in countries such as Australia, China, New Zealand, Argentina, Uruguay, and South Africa.

When I first went looking for organic wool suppliers in America, I didn't find many. Early producers of organic wool more often made the shift to organic production methods and became certified due to philosophical reasons rather than monetary incentives. Many domestic wool producers are resistant to the idea of transitioning to an organic production system and giving up the antibiotics and routine medicines to which they've grown accustomed. Frequently, they are also put off by the initial investment required in the organic conversion process.

It can take as long as three years for agricultural land to become certified organic. Furthermore, there are no allowances for the conversion of a flock of sheep from a non-organic system into an organic one. As a result, in order for a sheep producer to transition their entire flock to organic they must withhold lambs from the meat market, which means they lose money.

Sometimes a lack of firsthand knowledge and experience also contributes to the inertia associated with wool growers' slow transition to certified organic production systems. Agriculture is an inherently risky business, and many producers are afraid of adopting new technologies and production methods. Without appropriate incentives and demand from the market for both certified organic lamb and wool, it will likely be a slow transition.

In America, a crop like wool offers less incentive to go organic than, for instance, cotton. The farmer who converts his field to organic cotton will also reap a premium on the rotation crop, due to the high demand for organic produce. Wool farmers, on the other hand, are tied to the meat industry, and thus largely dependent upon the lamb market. The demand for organic lamb is not nearly as high as that of other organic meats and produce. Because wool is essentially a by-product of the lamb industry, it will require a surge in the demand for organic lamb to galvanize the domestic organic wool production base.

While there are small farms in the U.S. raising sheep organically for meat, we prefer to work with larger growers because they provide us with a more readily available and consistent product. In the face of low American supply (according to an OTA study, less than 20,000 pounds of organic wool were raised in the U.S. in 2005), I eventually began buying NOP accredited certified organic wool from Australia. It is simply easier for Australian sheep farmers to be organic. Their dry environment reduces the chance that the sheep will succumb to parasites that cull populations living in wetter environments. Australian sheep also enjoy vast grazing lands: about 18 acres per sheep. A dispersed flock has a relatively low risk of infection. Australian farmers can more easily do without veterinary medicines and conventional practices commonly practiced in other parts of the world.

As our production lots and running quantities grow, and with increased availability of fiber, we are now setting up offshore manufacturing relationships. This allows us to meet the needs of our clients in Asia. Another advantage of sourcing wools in Australia is its geographic proximity to the fiber processing plants and apparel manufacturing operations in Asia. This is important as we consider the overall global impact of our products and the importance of transportation in the equation.

Traditionally our customers are mission-driven companies focused on issues relating to sustainability, and social justice, and are often passionate and committed to using organic materials. Patagonia is a good example. In the '90s, Patagonia's decision to use only organic cotton in all of their cotton products had a tremendous impact on the industry. They held firm to their philosophy and to their code of ethics, and were able to get a number of vendors to switch along with them. Maggie's Organics is another mission-driven company we work with, supplying yarns for their organic wool socks.

In the past, the bulk of our business came from the outdoor market, which was simply a matter of circumstance. Now we get as many inquiries from larger companies, fashion and mainstream brands as we receive from outdoor apparel companies. We have also worked with a number of European brands whose interest in organic wool is significant.

When I work with companies interested in developing organic fiber lines, I approach them with an opportunity to broaden their organic offering and market segment. Previously, there was really only one option to produce and sell products made with certified organic fiber: organic cotton. Now we are able to offer another organic fiber and help these brands to expand their market. In addition to supplying organic wool raw materials, we also spend considerable amounts of time working with the sales and marketing departments helping them understand how to position their organic wool products and tell their story.

I still encounter the misconception that organic yarn or fabric is inferior. This is because early organic fibers and processing techniques were relatively crude. I have to educate designers about organic wool, show them product samples, and explain how we can help them offer beautiful, soft products that are more environmentally sensitive. Now I see designers excited by what is possible with new organic wool materials. Their inherent beauty and softness is apparent.

There is some reluctance to use organic materials because of the difference in price. Organic wool costs more than conventional wool for several reasons:

- Organic wool producers receive a higher price at the farm gate. Their costs of production are higher, primarily due to higher labor, management, and certification costs, but also because we feel it is important to pay them a premium for being good land stewards.

- The organic wool industry is very small relative to the overall wool industry and does not experience the economies of scale and resulting efficiencies of its conventional counterpart.

- Organic standards for livestock production inherently prohibit overgrazing. If the price of wool is low, loss of revenue cannot be made up by increasing production per unit of land. Such practices would put the natural system out of balance and ultimately lead to a loss of productivity. It could cause the animals to become sick. As demand spurs a growth in organic wool, we expect to see costs related to the second factor drop.

I expect that the organic wool supply will grow and mature, and the availability of products made with this wonderful material will become widely available through mainstream brands and merchants. Wool is a sophisticated and elegant material that deserves broader use. The time is not far away when major retailers will be carrying organic wools in addition to the organic cotton we are now seeing in many places.

———∞———

The Lowdown on Bamboo

Rich Delano, President
Bamboo Textiles

1015 E. Imperial Hwy, Suite C-7
Brea, CA 92821
www.spunbamboo.com
www.bambooapparel.com

B amboo. I find that the word itself helps sell the cloth made from it. Even before they touch silky bamboo fabric, people get excited, perhaps because of its association with pandas. Or Zen.

It turns out all those positive feelings, whatever their source, are absolutely justified. Bamboo is arguably one of the world's most sustainable resources. In particular, as a crop harvested for textile production, it compares favorably to trees and cotton.

From the production standpoint, bamboo is more efficient than trees. This grass grows up to one meter a day and continuously sends up new shoots, making it unnecessary to replant. Moreover, unlike trees, which can take up to 25 years to mature, it is ready to harvest after four years. Compared to trees, it does a superior job of removing carbon dioxide from the atmosphere, and one stand of bamboo releases 35 percent more oxygen than an equivalent stand of trees. Of course, we don't want to replace all trees with bamboo. By substituting bamboo for trees in our products, we can help save native forests from destruction.

Bamboo fiber has many of the physical properties that you see in cotton, and some more that you might wish you saw in cotton. For instance, it is antibacterial and has low absorbency; it is hypoallergenic and offers UV protection; it is incredibly soft and it sheds dirt well. In addition, bamboo cultivation taxes the environment far less than cotton. Notoriously, conventional cotton plants get doused with chemical pesticides and fertilizers. Bamboo needs none. Cotton fields that are not in rotation require fertilizers. Bamboo thrives in impoverished soil. Cotton is thirsty. Bamboo roots hold soil tight, retaining water in the watershed; furthermore, they mitigate water pollution due to high nitrogen consumption.

Yet for all its strengths, bamboo textile almost never made it to market. When I was first introduced to bamboo fiber, only a few fiber specialists had heard of it. The potential product was basically just sitting in a Chinese warehouse, waiting for an order. No one really knew what to do with it. Originally, I thought that I, too, would try to sell the yarn and fiber (that's what I had done for my old employer, a manufacturer of wood-based fiber), but I found potential buyers hard to convince. It took creating a bamboo t-shirt for them to realize that bamboo fiber could work for them.

After about six months of pitch after pitch but not a penny earned, my wife encouraged me to make some t-shirts. She reasoned that the t-shirt would be the perfect vehicle to show off the fiber's softness. My wife went down to the mall and bought a black, grey and white t-shirt from a popular brand. I sent those over to China to see whether they could make a similar product. As first tries usually do, our prototypes turned out terribly! Naturally, the bamboo textile didn't act like cotton. We had to learn how to deal with low stability and high shrinkage. When we found holes in our knits, we had to replace the needles on the knitting machines with sharper, smaller-gauge ones.

Even as I was trouble-shooting the manufacturing process, I was thinking about marketing. I wanted to make sure it was easy for business to find me. No one was going to travel from the four corners of the United States to visit a brick-and-mortar store, so I started to buy up domain names, about 60 of them in total: bambootextiles.com, bambooclothing.com, bamboobaby.com…. They were all available for seven dollars a piece. Then I set about spamming the entire bamboo community. I let them know that I had bamboo t-shirts, and I wanted to give them one for free—I'd even pay postage.

When my first order of 1,200 t-shirts arrived, I thought I might have a problem. The t-shirts were far from perfect. They were shrinking like crazy and not holding their shape. Still, I sent them out. People loved them. They wanted to know where they could buy one—but of course, they weren't for sale yet. Apart from the wonderful feel, I think people also responded to the novelty.

My second "lesson" in selling bamboo I learned from a trusted friend, Jack Chou, a successful author of books on entrepreneurship. I asked him, "How would you market this product if you were in my position?" He answered, "The best thing you can do right now is to not market it as a green material." He explained that if I started marketing it as green, I would pigeonhole myself, and my only customers would be "green freaks." I didn't want the environmental benefits of bamboo to become a stigma. I'd seen that happen to hemp. People think if you wear hemp you're smoking grass. That's an unfair stereotype that has been pinned on a nice product, but it's had a real impact on hemp's success. I didn't want similar associations to plague bamboo. So instead, I've chosen to sell the fiber on its inherent characteristics: It is silky soft. It breathes. It keeps you cool.

Though I finally got off to a promising start, I needed to start developing fabric. I kept pushing the envelope in anticipation of the moments when the "big guys" would get excited about bamboo and want to use it in many different applications. I knew they wouldn't want to wait a year for fabric development to catch up with their demand. I have developed some of the best bamboo fabric in the world; for example, French terry, thermal and denim. In addition, I've discovered that many different weights and textures can be achieved by blending bamboo with any fiber—I am currently experimenting with coconut and corn-based fiber, for instance. I have also poured my energy into investigating costs, shrink, hot-wash, and dyeing capabilities and soil release (i.e. the property that allows stains to leave the fabric). I knew that if I didn't do the research and development, someone else would.

Target bought fiber from my company and used it in their woven bed sheets, but while bamboo jerseys are rising to prominence, wovens are still quite rare. Weaving mills supplying giants like Chico's or Levi's run thousands and thousands of yards a day. Weaving machines cost millions of dollars, and the factories keep their machines running all night to make them pay for themselves. When I approach a mill and ask for 500 yards of woven for a research project, my contact laughs. On the other hand, 500 yards on a knitting machine is a reasonable order. Five hundred yards at five dollars per yard equals a price that makes experimentation possible. More wovens will appear as bamboo's popularity grows and companies decide it is worthwhile to invest in this outstanding fiber.

Bamboo fiber is delicate and has a very seductive drape and softness. Women love 100 percent bamboo fiber jersey as a layered garment or an undergarment, but manufacturers tend to blend it with cotton, Lycra or Spandex. This makes the yarn a little more resilient and lets the garment bounce back after wearing. My company has two brands, Spun Bamboo and Bamboo Apparel, and for those, we blend exclusively with organic cotton. My production customers or private label customers choose whether they want blends with cotton or organic cotton. If they're big customers, they almost always go for conventional cotton. It's an obvious way to whittle down the price, but it also increases the product's environmental impact.

Almost all bamboo comes out of China. I have had an office in China since my company's inception. Some people approach Chinese claims to sustainability with skepticism, either on the grounds of worker equity or environmental standards. I am very familiar with China; I've done production in practically every province. I know the Chinese way of thinking and working, and with the reciprocal suspicions that China and the U.S. harbor, but I've had nothing but good experiences in China.

American suspicion of Chinese environmental standards really has its roots in lack of transparency, caused by distance and cultural differences. Certainly these factors create abundant opportunities to dissimulate.

To my knowledge, bamboo is not yet being raised in America for textile purposes. I have been contacted by some American cotton farmers, however, who are considering cutting out half their cotton and growing bamboo in its place. Frankly, I don't feel that I can advise them on this matter. I don't know whether an

American farmer could compete with the Chinese prices, and I can't encourage someone to take a risk that, three years and 10 million dollars later, would prove not to pay off. That said, it would be wonderful if this possibility were investigated more fully. I know that there is some interest in creating a complete bamboo fiber product supply chain here in the U.S.

Bamboo textile is such a new product that it doesn't even have a widely accepted name yet. I've seen it called bamboo rayon, bamboo viscose, rayon from bamboo and just plain bamboo. It is important to establish a precise and standard descriptive vocabulary, both for the sake of creating a recognizable product and for the sake of keeping quality standards high.

Not all bamboo textiles are created alike, and it's important that consumers can choose which they want. There are two different methods of bamboo fiber production. One is more chemically intensive and the other is more mechanically intensive. During the former process, a non-toxic acid, n-methylmorpholine n-oxide (amine oxide) breaks down the bamboo stalks into a pulp. In the latter process, the bamboo is crushed to a powder, which is then mixed with water. In both cases, this cellulosic sludge is extruded to form the fiber. In feel and other characteristics, the end products yielded by these very different processes are indistinguishable, but the mechanical method is four to five times more expensive. I offer clients both products, and not surprisingly, they almost always go for the cheaper option.

I would love to see more support for the mechanically processed fiber, but in order for it to receive organic certification, we will need the U.S. government to treat bamboo fiber differently. Both kinds of bamboo fiber are brought in under the same tariff number and labeled "man-made fiber." As long as bamboo is considered man-made (rather than vegetable), existing organic standards do not apply. As a result, eschewing chemical processes does not offer the producer any commercial benefit. On the other hand, the U.S. government has a powerful monetary incentive not to change the label. Vegetable fibers enter the U.S. quota and duty-free. Even if it's not an organic label per se, applying some certification to differentiate between environmental standards of manufacture would be a crucial step toward making the most of its potential as an exemplary sustainable fiber.

In Defense of Truth and Beauty

Cheryl Kolander, Master Dyer and Founder
Aurora Silk

434 NE Buffalo Street
Portland, OR 97211
www.aurorasilk.com

I have been a professional natural dyer for 35 years. I create beautiful colors on silk using plants and one cultivated scale insect. At Aurora Silks, my Portland, Oregon-based workshop, I work at my dye vats daily, typically dyeing a pound or two of radiantly colored silk, hemp, or cotton by nightfall. I can proudly claim to have naturally dyed literally tons of fibers by hand. The length and breadth of my experience have established my reputation as one of a few senior natural dyers in the world.

My art, and therefore who I am, is an anachronism. These days, industrial chemical dye-works are the norm. In Europe, I have seen rivers run red and purple, orange and sickly green. Even worse are the petroleum works that manufacture the chemical colors. Their lack of concern for life is demonstrated by their other chemical products, such as pesticides and neurotoxins. A large area of Northern Italy was poisoned with dioxin in 1976, and a chemical cloud killed thousands in Bhopal, India in 1984. These industries are major global polluters. They are not the kind of industry that I want coloring my life.

It has taken fortitude and perseverance to stick by natural dyes in the face of widespread disinterest and ignorance, but there have been compelling reasons to continue my life's work. Some of them are personal. I love the unique smell of each dyestuff. Unlike art dyers who work with synthetics, I do not have to use a respirator. I love the magic of how white silk fibers plunged in a vat full of indigo solution emerge green, and then turn blue in the air. I love the precise, subtle, and complete spectrum of colors that I can create. As a whole, it is resplendent. Separately, each component is exquisite. But my art would not give me joy, and those colors would not appear so beautiful, if I knew that they endangered people and animals. I take pride in the fact that what I create and how I support my family is achieved through a business that is ecologically sound.

I am an anachronism, but I think the time is ripe for more people like me who choose to make, buy, and wear natural dyes. Surely there are many people who value beauty, but who also realize that true beauty cannot be achieved through ugly means. I say "surely," though I am continually disappointed by the lack of a market for natural dyes. Because of the dearth of consumers, we are in danger of losing valu-able knowledge about natural dyes.

There seem to be many misconceptions about the nat-ural dye industry. I'm afraid that they stop consumers from demanding natural dyes and investors from funding the industrialization of natural dye-works.

One comment I hear repeatedly about natural dyes is, "The colors are all blah." People who say this really have no experience with natural dyes and must be relying on spurious hearsay. I assure you that it is possible to create a full rainbow using no toxic or poisonous chemicals. I have 120 numbered artisan colors and another two dozen industrial formulations that I routinely produce and know intimately. If a designer came to me and wanted to design a specific color to distinguish his or her collection from anyone else's, I could make that color. I could probably develop four different ways to make that color.

Detractors of natural dyes are quick to criticize their fastness. Someone (the synthetic dye industry, maybe?) is spreading a rumor that natural dyes tend to bleed and fade. A successful dye is colorfast. A good dyer, one who knows the right ratio of dyestuff to mordant, will create trustworthy colors. I dye all of my own clothes. They look great, wash after wash after wash. In fact, one of the real assets of well-done natural dyes is their tendency to increase in luminosity! In India, indigo reaches its full potential after a year of being worn and washed. For proof that natural dyes last and last, visit the textile department of any major museum. You'll see a stunning range of gorgeous textiles that are still brilliant after hundreds of years: Louis XIV silks, Renaissance velvets, Chinese Imperial robes, Japanese kimonos, Coptic fragments, Peruvian weavings, Indonesian ikats, and the Unicorn Tapestries. All were naturally dyed (remember, before 1856, all textiles were dyed naturally). All are still exquisitely beautiful. These days, most people throw out their clothes after a couple of years at the most. Natural dyes are colorfast enough for the demands of our modern lifestyles.

Another claim that irks me is that natural dyes are difficult to produce consistently. Granted, obtaining consistent colors takes skill and education. However, natural dyeing skills can be taught just like any other skill. Think about the chemists and engineers on whom most of the world relies to create synthetic colors. Those scientists are highly and expensively trained. The average person could not walk into a color lab, throw some chemicals around and create consistent colors either! A considerable amount of knowledge about natural dyes has been accumulated empirically. This information could be easily scientifically developed, refined, and cataloged so that more people could learn to execute the best techniques. It just takes interest from researchers and the academic community.

Lastly, people claim that natural dyes are just as bad for the environment as synthetic dyes. Please! All synthetic dyes are made from coal tar, one of the most carcinogenic substances on the planet. The mordants used by natural dyers are all salts of minerals needed by the body: iron, copper, tin and alum. Efficient dyers use them in very small amounts. Most of these metal salts are used at the ratio of 3:100 by weight of fabric. The ratio of the actual metal ion to fabric is just 1:200, and these ions become fixed to the fabric-dye combination. Almost nothing is discharged, even using standard machinery. Aurora Silk hopes to attract investment in a state-of-the-art industrial, natural dye-works that emits zero percent discharge in Portland. I am also developing a line of no-mordant colors, such as my Indigo "Peace" blue and "Therapeutic Gold." My next book, In My Grandma's Garden, is a fun exploration of no-mordant colors for kids. You can use them for Easter eggs!

Nowhere in the world do industrial natural dye-works, which could handle a department store-sized order, still exist. This was not always the case. Until very recently, India, Indonesia, Pakistan, Egypt and all of Central and South America were dyeing naturally on an industrial scale. (In the industrial setting, the artist's 10-gallon pots and painstaking attention are replaced with a giant stainless steel machine with rollers that take the fabric through an enclosed dye bath.) In those regions, vestiges of equipment and expertise still remain. Industrial natural dye-works and printworks used to exist in New York City, too. Their swatch books can be found in library archives. Industrial natural dyeworks could be resuscitated within a decade, if not half that. Given all the advantages and promise of natural dyes, one would expect investors to be knocking on my door. They're not, a fact I attribute partly to the rampant misconceptions I have mentioned, and partly to the fact that two major, basic challenges need to be overcome. Dealing with these challenges now will yield the highest return, both in terms of ethics and profits.

The first and probably the most serious impediment to the future of natural dyeing is the decrease in the supply of natural dyestuffs around the world. As synthetic dyes have taken over, the market for indigo, logwood, cochineal, madder, woad and brazilwood has dwindled to almost nothing. At present, not enough natural dyestuffs exist to serve a vigorous market. The good news is, in some cases, production could be quickly reenergized. A field of indigo, for instance, could yield a crop in one year. In as little as two years, cochineal plantation workers could be harvesting the little red bugs from the cacti they live on. In the case of dyes extracted from trees, however, a little more planning is needed. Logwood trees, which give a rich black, take twenty years to mature. The sooner we start, the better! Of course investing in the cultivation of these kinds of dye crops would be the wise thing to do because, in contrast to petroleum, which is the basic component of synthetic dyes and a finite resource, plants and animals can be managed sustainably.

Investing in the dye industry would provide a wonderful opportunity for a benign income source for many people in historically impoverished areas. Almost exclusively, the strongest, clearest, and fastest natural dyes—the ones I depend on—come from the Third World. Why? Natural dyes are captured sunlight, in essence, and there's a whole lot more sun in the tropics. Ideally, investors should support the already established natural dye producers, which are owned and staffed by citizens of those countries. Given the opportunity, these producers will expand to meet the world demand for quality color. Madder, an herb whose root yields red dye, would make a better alternative to poppies in the fields of Afghanistan. The Kandahar Valley once produced the finest madder in the world, hence the expensive rugs from that region.

Clearly, the solution to dwindling raw materials is straightforward and broadly beneficial for people on both the manufacturing and consumer end of the production chain. It just takes vision and capital to make it happen.

Yes, natural dyes will cost slightly more than conventional ones. (They add the cost of two latte grandes to the price of a new shirt.) What should be a justifiable markup makes most consumers balk instead of buy. There is a small sector of super-sensitive individuals whose health and environmental concerns prompt them to buy natural. I remain optimistic that the rest of the populace will learn to care about the benefits of natural dyes and spend accordingly. We must first see through the fraud that cheap is better. It may seem cheaper to engineer an artificial spectrum of color from the basic building block of petroleum's hydrocarbon chain, but, really, the only one getting rich is the company that manufactures them. The real cost is exorbitant: death, pollution and diminished resources.

Consumers, though first seduced by cheap prices, can learn to value quality again. I remember when polyester came on the market. Suddenly, you couldn't buy cotton. Eventually, chiefly for the reason of comfort, consumers demanded more cotton. Even when 100 percent cotton was reintroduced at a higher price, people paid it. I hope that the kind of consumer who now passes over synthetic blends for the quality of pure wool, pure silk, pure linen and pure cotton will soon also be looking to read "100 percent natural dyes" on the tags of their purchases.

One more piece of the puzzle has to be in place before the natural dye industry can gain popularity. Natural dye professionals must set standards for quality work and have one or several channels for certification. The adoption of standards and certification will serve two critical purposes: first, it will combat the prejudices that many people harbor concerning natural dyes by indicating the quality of colors; second, it will ensure sound ethical and ecological practices. In response to this need I developed Tyria, a certification system named after the biblically attested dyer Lydia of Tyre, patroness of Paul the Apostle. Tyria rates color-dye-mordant combinations based on their fastness to washing and light. It also recently framed ecological impact and health benefits ratings for each dye-mordant-color.

Much remains to be done to transform natural dyeing into the industry that the world needs. However, we certainly won't be creating this industry in a vacuum. We have the wisdom from thousands of years of dyeing to guide us. We also have a growing number of consumers who can envision a more beautiful world.

Color, Magic, and Modern Alchemy

John Patrick, Founder
Organic

johnpatrickorganic@gmail.com

In 2000, I bought a 10,000-square-foot abandoned warehouse with no roof in downtown Albany, New York. Why? I had no idea. Instinct? Madness? Or maybe a combination of the two? It had been an upholstery shop for many years and was the first building designed and built in Albany after the horrific Triangle Shirtwaist Factory fire in New York City in 1911. I felt it had textile energy and was a relevant place for my work and archives.

Each floor is filled with different periods of my work. All the things that make the fashion business happen—samples, rolls of cloth, scraps—take up space. My little brother is always saying it would be nice to get the piles on the floor "off the floor!" The first piece I made for Organic happened by accident. My friend Ann Marie Gardner, who was writing for Organic Style Magazine, asked me to design something.

I thought about it and said, "Let's make an apron." We made it in organic canvas. The magazine shot it. Rural Residence, a store in Hudson, New York, took the orders, and the phone rang off the hook with people who wanted the "sexy apron." I realized then that I could incorporate a lot of things that didn't fit into fashion and design, make them, tell a story, and do the right thing. I started to understand that there was a way I could make things that I truly loved, not just racks of clothing that was disposable after a season. Why not do exquisite embroideries in organic cloth? "Make less" and "better and slowly" became my mantras – it is impossible to do everything.

Still, I wanted lots of excitement. So I started wandering around in Lima, Peru. I met a vegetarian taxi driver, Victor Zarate, and told him of plans for this organic company. He became my assistant and is now the general manager of the company. He will be attending the next Organic Exchange meeting in Ecuador, and I trust him with my life. Victor and I weren't trying to make things to impress anyone. We were just having fun and trying to do the next important thing.

When I first started my Organic collection, I only wanted color "that came off the animal," as in shades of wool that came down from the highlands of the Peruvian border. We found a weaver, Maria Condor, who was working in the Highlands. I selected colors for a blanket I called the "personal travel blanket." There were seven colors from pure cream to dark gray, brown, and black. People who knew me said, "Turn it into a collection!"

As I moved on to scarves, I was insistent on "no color." Everything was the color of oatmeal. While traveling in Berlin that first season, women in fur coats said they loved the styles, but that "the fabrics were too poor." Ironically, I knew I had succeeded. Soon after, the scarves were bought by Penelope, a store in Brescia, Italy.

For the next collection, I moved on to hats. While rooting around at the Vanves flea market in Paris, I found a fold-up safari canvas hat, which you can use as a water bowl. I focused on water because I wanted to show the collection next to the reservoir in New York's Central Park. Water awareness meets Fashion Week! For this collection, we explored the use of indigo. I had been seeing artisanal, natural dyes used by the people from the Highlands in Peru, but they always looked too pink or too strong. While wander-ing around Lima, searching for something that would catch my eye, I saw an exhibit of spinning wheels made from recycled bicycle wheels, and cotton yarns dyed in the most sophisticated colors. After tracking down the artist, Ricardo Calmet, we met in a coffee shop. I wanted to see where he did his work and how it was done. Days later, we ended up in a workshop in a Lima neighborhood. There were so many fascinating things: yarn ideas spun together, lit-tle spinning wheels made from the bicycle wheels, and many other experiments Ricardo had been

working on for years. Together, we went to the coun-
tryside to see where the cotton was dyed. I saw colors made from rattan root and cochinilla, among
many other plants. The colors and process were so
beautiful. They were basic and sophisticated at once.

The modern Silk Road took yet another turn. In
Ricardo Calmet, we found the color guru of the
movement! His commitment, singleness of purpose,
and unselfish sharing of his knowledge was infec-
tious. I told him that he was the best I had ever seen
and that he should make a "color box" every season,
so that potential buyers could order and use it as a
reference. He promptly did, and it has proved a useful tool. As we speak, he is dyeing t-shirts knit from
jungle cotton for me.

Another color pioneer is Anco Snape, a Dutchman I
met at the Organic Exchange conference in Utrecht,
October 2006. He has an encyclopedic knowledge of
the history of the madder root from the past 500
years. He references alchemy. It is fascinating to
think of a colorist from the Middle Ages walking into
a village and gathering people around him as he
transforms a piece of handspun wool or flax from its
natural color into a vibrant vermilion, much like
Ricardo Calmet and all of the incredible people who
have shared their magic with me.

What Does Planting Tomatoes Have to Do with Fashion?

Natalie Chanin, Designer and Founder
Alabama Chanin

6534 County Road 200
Florence, AL 35633
www.alabamachanin.com

The Alabama tomato is truly a wonder. It takes on the color of the deep red soil, and the taste borders on sweet and tart. I grew up eating these tomatoes straight out of my grandparents' garden in Florence, Alabama, and after having lived in Europe for more than 20 years, I still think Alabama tomatoes are the best in the world. So when I moved back to my hometown in Florence, to a place called Lovelace Crossroads, I was eager to have a garden and grow my own.

I quickly realized I could not remember the details of how to plant a tomato, so I consulted Mr. Jay Arnet, an 87-year-old family friend who has the most beautiful kitchen garden. He taught me how to lovingly remove the bottom branches from the seedlings, dig a hole that seemed too big, fill it with compost and water the plants. They produced the tomatoes that filled our stomachs all summer and became the basis for our soups in the winter. Thanks to Mr. Arnet, the plants thrived and our cupboard was filled with cans of stewed tomatoes.

I was a little shocked that I had lost this very basic knowledge of how to grow my own food. On its most immediate level, growing food literally connects you to roots and earth, but it also connects you with the skills and traditions that farmer families have used forever as they tilled the land to produce fruit, vegetables and—in this area—cotton.

Planting a garden after coming back to Alabama was more than just a way to celebrate my homecoming; it was also a way to immerse myself in the "domestic arts," which I prefer to call "living arts." I realized that here in my community, activities such as sewing, gardening, cooking and quilting have never just been tasks. They're artful endeavors that allow for independence, a way to take direct responsibility for quality of life, and simultaneously they create a bond between individuals and community, between past and present.

In our community, one of the many ways women bonded was at quilting bees. These gatherings tapped into the region's long, rich history of textile work and celebrated skills that were passed from generation to generation. Unfortunately the value of these skills has diminished and often they are no longer passed on.

That's one reason why I returned home to Alabama—to create a collection of clothing that preserved and reinvigorated those unique hand-sewing traditions, which I learned at the feet of grandmothers, mother and aunts. I also wanted to use recycled materials and employ age-old production techniques.

I never imagined that this idea would receive so much attention from the fashion and business worlds, especially during a time when U.S. textile production was moving in the opposite direction. Instead of going overseas, I worked with about 200 skilled artisans who became revered by fashion insiders for their elaborately embellished, hand-sewn garments that are sold in more than 60 stores around the world.

Alabama Chanin is still inspired by local sewing traditions. I was recently reminded of how precious these techniques are when I stumbled upon a piece of handwork made by my grandmother. It was a pillowcase with intricate needlework sewn onto a flour sack. I could just make out the company's imprint as a shadow on the fabric, and as I examined this lovely piece of work, I thought: It's incredible. She spent hours and hours—probably over the course of months—making something from a piece of fabric that today would be thrown into the garbage.

The men and women who raised me were artisans who used readily available materials to create objects, both decorative and functional, which enriched our lives. These items were never considered anything extraordinary, and the people who made them were humble about their work. Unfortunately, there are fewer and fewer people who can make such heirlooms. Most of those who stitch for us grew up learning to sew from family members, so it was no surprise when at one point we had three generations of the same family working together.

By encouraging these handwork traditions, Alabama Chanin is also hoping to sustain the identity of this stretch of land at the foot of the Appalachian Mountains. While most people talk about sustainability in reference to chemicals or materials and their effect on the environment, I also think sustainability depends on nurturing the skills necessary to manipulate local materials into well-designed objects. I believe it's essential that we respect the sanctity of our traditions and the skilled workers who keep them alive.

Whether planting a tomato or embroidering a napkin, staying connected to these traditions allows us to also cherish them. Handwork requires respect for everyday materials and helps us imagine their potential. It also forces us to use our resources wisely. The people in my community learned to use what they had on hand and make the most of it, especially during The Great Depression. One of my favorite examples of this ethic is the way women used to find the red thread that they used for quilting. At the time, red thread was costly and hard to come by. After the men had smoked or chewed the contents of their Red Man Tobacco pouches, women would take the coarse cotton tobacco bags, unravel the red thread and use it in their sewing projects. This attitude that all things have potential continues to inspire me. It's·an ethic that I try to remember every day as I build my company and design my collections.

Like my original tomato garden, my company has grown. In addition to garments, we now make home furnishings and jewelry. I'm still able to pursue the original vision of working with outstanding artisans and recycled materials to make beautiful products, but we're also trying to do more than just sell things.

A big part of our mission is to make sure these wonderful skills get passed on. We try to spend as much time focusing on workshops and lectures as we do on producing products and garments. In the Spring of 2008, I will publish a book that teaches our techniques and offers patterns and inspiration.

These are just a few small ways that I'm hoping to teach more people about the living arts. When we think about how to make a bowl, a dress, or a chair, the process is often shrouded in mystery. Instead we buy one at the store. But that simple purchase has much bigger ramifications. It creates more distance between us and the power we have to create for ourselves.

It's my hope that these craft traditions, like planting those tomato plants, will allow us to reap the fruit of our labor and talent while helping us participate more deeply in the rhythms of our everyday lives. Ultimately, I hope the living arts will also re-establish our communities as sustainable, dynamic and inspiring places to live.

SECTION 5:

THE SCIENCE OF CHANGE

Eco-Effective Fashion

Dr. Michael Braungart, Partner
McDonough Braungart Design Chemistry

700 E. Jefferson Street, Third Floor
Charlottesville, VA 22902
www.mbdc.com
Professor

Universität Lüneburg
Scharnhorststraße 1
Postfach 2440
21314 Lüneburg, Germany
www.uni-lueneburg.de/adresse.php
Founder

EPEA International Umweltforschung GmbH
Feldstrasse 36
D – 20357
Hamburg, Germany

In this material world, textiles are everywhere. From the clothes we wear to the fabrics we walk on, textiles of varying colors, designs and materials surround us. Although beautiful, their production, use and disposal are generally very hazardous for both human and environmental health.

Worldwide, more than 32 million people are employed in clothing production and its related activities. Especially in developing countries, this industry, which accounts for 42 percent of exported consumer goods, has the potential to serve as an engine for economic growth and industrialization. At the same time, it has the distinct ability to injure natural and social systems.

Many have tried to decrease the textile industry's impact on the environment and human health. However, in essence, these eco-efficient attempts to be good only go so far. Water, air and soil are still polluted. Energy and natural resources are still wasted. Humans are still coming in contact with toxic materials. Clearly, less bad is not good!

In order to truly benefit the environment, instead of eco-efficient solutions, the textile industry needs to implement eco-effective strategies which regenerate the economy, society and the environment. Rather than merely seeking to reduce toxins and waste, eco-effective strategies admit no toxins or waste. Instead, they use only "healthy" materials, that is, fibers and chemicals that can become nutrients for future textiles. Instead of focusing on the end of the pipe, eco-effective thinking envisions production as a closed loop.

One revolutionary eco-effective approach is Cradle to Cradle Design. Cradle to Cradle Design holds that rigorous science and design give us the tools to move beyond mere sustainability. Why sustain when you could thrive? Nature has devised productive systems that flourish. With science providing the understanding of physical laws and design serving as the signal of human intention, Cradle to Cradle Design creates industry that, like nature, continuously propagates life and growth. This paradigm claims three basic principles: waste equals food, use current solar income, and celebrate diversity.

With a practical, strategic expression of an eco-effective philosophy, Cradle to Cradle Design defines the framework for designing products and the industrial processes that turn materials into nutrients, by enabling their perpetual flow within one of two distinct metabolisms. This is an important distinction: the nutrients are flowing in their respective metabolisms, not the processes. The products may also, but "nutrients" refers more to the materials that make up the product.

The first of these two distinct metabolisms is the biological metabolism—the cyclical processes of nature. The biological metabolism is a network of interdependent organisms and natural processes. It comprises complementary nutrient needs and metabolic by-products. Nutrients perpetually cycle through the system. Materials that flow optimally through the biological metabolism are called biological nutrients. As defined for Cradle to Cradle products, biological nutrients are biodegradable (or otherwise naturally degradable) materials that pose no immediate or eventual hazard to living systems. They can be used and safely returned to the environment. Products conceived as biological nutrients are called products of consumption. They are designed for safe and complete return to the environment, where they become nutrients of healthy living systems. Detergents, "disposable" packaging and products that dissipate during use (shoe soles, brake pads, etc.) are prime products of consumption.

The other, the technical, metabolism, is an industrial model that circulates valuable materials in a closed loop of production, use, recovery and reproduction. The technical metabolism is the Cradle to Cradle system for industrial production of primarily synthetics and mineral resources. It is modeled on the biological metabolism: no waste, only nutrients that perpetually circulate in closed-loop cycles. A technical nutrient is a material that remains safely in a closed loop system of manufacture, recovery, and reuse (the technical metabolism), maintaining its highest value through many product life cycles. Technical nutrients are used in products of service, which are durable goods. The product is used by the customer but owned by the manufacturer, either formally or in effect. Washing machines, automobiles and television sets are products of service that could be designed for perpetual return, reprocessing and re-use.

Within both the biological and technical metabolisms, materials function as nutrients. Cradle to Cradle Design uses only those materials that flow safely in one or the other of these discrete metabolisms.

Along with my colleagues at EPEA and MBDC, I have worked with companies to implement the concepts of Cradle to Cradle discussed above.

Climatex® Lifecycle upholstery fabric—created in collaboration with EPEA Internationale Umweltforschung, MBDC and Rohner Textil, Switzerland—is an example of a product whose constituent materials were designed to be biological nutrients. Before eco-effective optimization of the product, trimmings from the mill were classified as hazardous waste requiring special and expensive disposal. Moreover, workers in the mill dealt with toxic chemicals on a daily basis. Most critically, the mill polluted the local river to such an extreme that the government asked it to cease production.

To reform the mill's production processes, new dyes were sought to replace the toxic ones. From a selection of 1,600 dye formulations acquired from 60 dye suppliers, EPEA identified 16 that met both the desired technical and environmental specifications. The completely biodegradable and compostable fabric is made from natural fibers, including wool from free-ranging, humanely sheared New Zealand sheep and ramie, a tall, fibrous plant grown in Asia.

After Cradle to Cradle re-engineering, waste material from the mill could be made into felt to be used as garden mulch and in the cultivation of strawberries, cucumbers and a wide range of other plants. Workers no longer had to handle toxic chemicals. And the space used for storing toxic materials was renovated into staff offices and a lounge. Tests registered cleaner river water downstream of the mill than upstream.

A similar design process is used to create products that are also technical nutrients. Alain Duval, president of Victor Innovatex, a contract fabric-producing company, sought to differentiate his brand by focusing on new technologies and environmental responsibility. Victor collaborated with EPEA and MBDC to develop a technical nutrient upholstery fabric called Victor Eco-Intelligent Polyester (EIP).

Although historically preferred by environmentalists because of its recyclability, the production, use and recycling of polyester have negative consequences. Almost half of the world's yearly production of synthetic fibers is polyester, an amount that totals around 11 million tons. The main catalyst used in polyester production is antimony, a known carcinogen and a toxin that affects the heart, lungs, liver and skin. By-products of antimony cause chronic bronchitis and emphysema. They also pollute waterways. Polyester recycling is actually often downcycling: The polymer quality degenerates, limiting its future applicability in other products. Recycling polyester reproduces many of the toxic events that are integral to conventional polyester manufacturing.

EIP is a different story. By starting with the design process at the molecular level, EPEA and MBDC were able to substitute dangerous chemicals with healthy dyestuffs and auxiliary chemicals—including a new catalyst to replace antimony. (In the end, we green-lighted 15 out of the 57 original chemicals.) But the benefits of EIP do not end at production. EIP is designed to be safely recycled into new fabric at the end of its life, with none of the hazardous by-products of traditional polyester recycling. Since the Cradle to Cradle revamping, Victor has defined its niche in the competitive marketplace. It's providing providing a healthy example for the textile trade and a signal of hope for human industry.

The major push for eco-effectiveness has occurred in industrialized countries. However, developing countries account for approximately 50 percent of world textile exports and 70 percent of world clothing exports. They also contribute a disproportionate amount (81 percent) of textile sector water pollution. A combination of economic, political and social factors has resulted in a technology gap between textile operations in developing nations and those in industrialized nations. As a result, developing nations implement considerably fewer sound technologies. To improve the situation in these countries, I have worked with the United Nations Industrial Development Organization to base investments on eco-effectiveness. The infrastructure set in place by UNIDO's Cleaner Production program, as well as Public Private Partnership activities and UNIDO's Innovation Initiatives, serve as valuable tools in encouraging the effective implementation of Cradle to Cradle strategies and the creation of a regenerative textile sector in developing countries.

Despite its shortcomings, the textile industry has enormous potential to positively affect economic, social and environmental conditions in industrial and developing countries. In Asia, the ability of the textile industry to fuel economic development and lead the integration of developing countries into a global economy has already become apparent. At the same time, an ever-growing number of consumers concerned about the environment, health and social issues provide an increasing market for responsibly produced textiles. More and more, eco-labeling mechanisms and corporate codes of conduct are providing a way to push this demand deeper into the textile supply chain. The technological framework of Cradle to Cradle offers ways to meet these demands, while providing advantages in terms of cost, quality and market.

Given the enormity of its scale and influence, the textile sector could benefit from a modern restoration. It is a prime opportunity for the employment of the Cradle to Cradle framework to provide a longer-term vision of a sustainability and an economically vibrant industry. If done right, the textile industry can be a positive force. It can support and benefit society and the environment, while prospering economically.

The Consequences of Chemicals

Dr. Lauren Heine, Ph.D., Director of Applied Science
Green Blue Institute

600 E. Water St. Suite C
Charlottesville, VA 22902
www.greenblue.org

While a deft pencil or watercolor sketch determines the silhouette of a garment, it represents only part of the design process. Bringing a piece of apparel off the page and into the store requires chemistry. The textile industry uses chemicals to remove waxes or oils from fibers, to break down cellulose, to lubricate fibers during spinning, to color cloth and to give cloth a light-fast or stain-proof coating—among other things. Though generally unacknowledged, the quality of the chemistry determines in large part the feel, look and durability of the finished article. Chemistry is also important in determining how safe the apparel manufacturing process is to humans and ecosystems.

In its zealousness to please the eye, the fashion industry has tended to ignore the consequences of chemistry. It can lead to tragic events. In February 2006, a four-year-old boy died after swallowing the charm from a "silver" bracelet that came with a pair of Reebok children's shoes. While the Consumer Products Safety Commission advises that jewelry sold in the U.S. contain no more than 0.06 percent lead, the charm was 99 percent lead. Clearly, this incident tarnished Reebok's image.

At Green Blue Institute, a nonprofit founded by William McDonough and Michael Braungart, we believe that a product is truly successful when it:

- Meets market requirements

- Has positive social effects (for individuals and communities)

- Is safe for human and ecological health

- Is sourced from renewable or repeatedly recycled materials

- Is sourced from renewable energy

- Is designed for safe, productive return to nature or industry

- Is recovered and recycled at the highest quality after use

This is consistent with what McDonough and Braungart call the Cradle to Cradle Design vision.

This essay focuses on what is meant by "safe for human and ecological health," and "designed for productive return to nature or industry." To simplify the discussion, I refer to these two ideas combined as "material health." Material health refers to chemicals, materials and products that are safe and healthy for humans and the environment during their full life cycle, with a focus on design for safe, productive return to nature or industry. This essay also includes some suggested strategies for integrating material health into the supply chain.

Achieving material health depends on companies taking the initiative to: know their materials, know the impacts of these materials and chemicals over their full life cycle; choose green chemicals and materials, and keep the big picture in mind to support sustainable material flows.

KNOW YOUR MATERIALS

Chemical and material supply chains can be long, and it is often difficult to know exactly what chemicals are in the materials you wish to use in a product; chemicals can both serve and destroy life. Examining the material health of your design palette is worth the effort.

Knowing your materials involves an inventory of all the chemicals that comprise them – ideally down to 100 parts per million (100 ppm or 0.01 percent). If it is not initially possible to identify components to 100 ppm, then identifying all chemicals used in products and processes to 1000 ppm (0.1 percent) is a good start.

Strategies for knowing your materials include:

- Requiring full ingredient disclosure from suppliers under confidentiality agreements.

- Creating Restricted Substances Lists (RSLs or X-Lists) and requiring suppliers to sign affidavits that these chemicals are not intentionally added or present, or are above a certain concentration. RSLs are useful in driving change through the supply chain. While they are not the most effective tool at greening chemistry overall, they do help to eliminate some of the worst actors. RSLs begin the process of exploring more favorable alternatives.

- Implementing a P-list (Preferred or Positive List) of chemicals. In contrast to specifying to suppliers what chemicals or materials you don't want, it is useful to specify exactly what you do want. Once a material or chemical is well characterized (i.e. its material health attributes are known), and it is considered benign with respect to human and environmental health, it can be added to the P-list. For example, a manufacturer may source organic cotton or polyester made with benign and/or antimony-free catalysts and seek to develop a product line based on these fibers.

KNOW THE IMPACT OF THESE MATERIALS AND CHEMICALS OVER THEIR FULL LIFECYCLE

Designers and manufacturers can prevent harmful consequences by understanding the inherent hazards and potential for exposure associated with chemicals and materials over their life cycle. Knowing the potential impacts of chemicals and materials is a challenge. Companies that employ toxicologists and/or human and environmental health and safety experts can assess chemicals in-house. Others may need to consult outside expertise.

The U.S. Environmental Protection Agency's Design for the Environment Program has a saying that, "if it is not in your formulation, you don't have to worry about it." This motto reflects common sense and speaks to the difference—critical in the world of chemical, material and product assessment—between risk and inherent hazard.

Risk is a function of hazard and exposure. In a world where we choose to take on risks every day, we gamble that by adequately avoiding exposure (to freezing temperatures, toxic chemicals, speeding cars, etc.) we can avoid harm. But exposure controls can and do fail. Dramatic examples include the Bhopal Disaster of 1984. This catastrophe killed nearly 3,000 people initially and 15,000 later from injuries related to the accidental release of methyl isocyanate from a Union Carbide plant. There are also more insidious and less acute affects, such as the bioaccumulation in our bodies of chemicals used to retard flame in fabrics and electronics. In both cases, the exposure is unintentional but could have been avoided if the chemicals used had been selected based on low inherent hazard and low bioaccumulation potential.

Chemical hazard includes toxicity. Toxicity is the adverse effect of a chemical, physical or biological agent to living organisms and ecosystems. Toxins are substances with relatively high degrees of potency. Toxicity depends on the organism, the dose and the route of exposure. Salt, for instance, is not typically considered a toxin; nevertheless, in the right (or rather, wrong) circumstance, it has toxicity. Hazard can also include potential adverse effects to ecosystem functions at the local and global levels. Examples of local adverse effects on ecosystems in the textile industry come from wet processing effluent discharged into rivers and streams, resulting in dead zones due to effluent aquatic toxicity and biological oxygen demand, and areas where chemicals are found that are considered to disrupt the normal reproductive development of fish, such as degradates of branched chain nonylphenol ethoxylate surfactants used for cleaning. At the global level, impacts include depletion of the stratospheric ozone layer due to emissions of chlorofluorocarbons, and climate change due to emissions of CO_2 and other greenhouse gases. Hazard can also be associated with the feedstock used to create the chemicals. For example, petroleum-based materials depend on a non-renewable resource. Heavy metals such as chromium and cadmium, while capable of making bright and vibrant dyes, can pose a threat wherever they appear in the product lifecycle: during mining, use of the dye in dye wastewater, or as a result of composting or incineration. It is important to consider hazards across a chemical's lifecycle, as exemplified by those azo dyes that are both synthesized from, and degraded to, genotoxic (i.e. harmful to DNA) aromatic amines.

Hazards include but are not limited to:

• Acute toxicity to humans

• Chronic health effects (e.g., carcinogenicity and other adverse effects on development, reproduction, neurological, immune, endocrine or other organ systems)

• Skin, eye or respiratory irritation or sensitization

• Toxicity to aquatic and terrestrial organisms

• Global effects (e.g., climate change, ozone depletion)

• Depletion of renewable or non-renewable resources

• Bioaccumulation of chemicals in living creatures

• Persistence of toxic chemicals; accumulation of waste that needs transport, takes up space in landfills, and has the potential to leach or otherwise escape to the environment.

Another famous saying is, "the dose makes the poison" which is attributed to Theophrastus Phillippus Aureolus Bombastus von Hohenheim, aka Paracelcus (1493 - 1541). Paracelcus noted that, "All substances are poisons; there is none which is not a poison. The right dose differentiates a poison from a remedy." He was right; however, newer science has determined that it is not just dose but timing that's critical. Effects may depend on the stage of the organism's development and the potential for synergy with other chemicals or conditions in the environment (temperature, stress, etc.). In addition, small doses may have different, delayed or poorly understood effects. There is still much to learn about the mechanisms of action of endocrine disruption and the toxicology of nanoparticles.

CHOOSE GREEN CHEMICALS AND MATERIALS

Green chemistry is defined as the "design of products and processes that reduce or eliminate the use and/or generation of hazardous substances." (Anastas and Warner, 1999.) A set of principles helps chemists understand and develop green chemicals. Green chemistry is referred to as green and sustainable chemistry in some countries, where green tends to imply an emphasis on the environment, while sustainable is considered more inclusive of human health and social well-being. But either way, as awareness and impetus for green and sustainable chemistry grows, there is a growing palette of chemicals and materials from which to choose.

Strategies for choosing green chemicals and materials include:

Developing P-lists of chemicals or materials

This approach is recommended as a strategy for knowing your materials, i.e. specifying materials or chemicals identified as positive or preferred. In order to create a P-list, it is necessary to evaluate the available chemicals and material options and to determine what qualifies as preferred. Sometimes selection of preferred chemicals or materials is made relatively easy by assuming a certain level of achievement based on membership in an organization, or certification to a standard or eco-label. For example, members of the Ecological and Toxicological Association of Dyes and Organic Pigments Manufacturers (ETAD) must agree that they will not make or sell colorants with heavy metals that have impurities above certain trace limits or that are capable of releasing aromatic amines that are known or suspected carcinogens. Manufacturers who have had their colorants assessed (in products that have been certified to standards or eco-labels) will typically provide information on the colorants that meet the criteria of a variety of standards and eco-labels around the world (e.g., the Global Organic Textile Standard). The Standard for Sustainable Contract Furnishing Fabrics (soon to be released as a joint standard between the Association for Contract Textiles, NSF International, and Green Blue Institute) will also set levels of achievement that raise the bar and push toward the ideal of material health.

Chemicals and materials can also be benchmarked against the 12 Principles of Green Chemistry and against the ideal of low inherent hazard across all hazard endpoints. They can be compared to other chemicals that perform the same function, in order to identify "best in class." Sometimes the best in class comes close to the ideal, but in other cases even the best in class can be considered potentially problematic, for instance, the case of fluorinated finishes that protect fibers. The choice to use the best of a problematic class is difficult because the manufacturer may be torn between performance demands and available technology. The trick is to ensure that the decision does not perpetuate the status quo but rather continues to drive demand for the development of benign technologies.

Design healthy alternatives with suppliers who apply green chemistry principles

Chemists are creative. The best will argue that they can create pretty much whatever type of molecule a client wants. However, they need assurance that their R&D efforts will be rewarded. Manufacturers who explain their concerns regarding material health to suppliers will often find them "all ears." If they perform well, materials designed with respect for human and environmental health, safety, and sustainability will be desirable to many customers. Therefore, such demands may be viewed as drivers for innovation.

Look for emerging green chemistries and technologies, which change quickly in the material world

The newly widespread interest in material health has created an intellectually exciting set of problems for top industry and academic talent to tackle. The Presidential Green Chemistry Challenge (PGCC) Awards, the only Presidential-level awards in the field of chemistry in the United States, are given to innovative green chemicals and materials. May the recent winners serve as inspiration!

DuPont produced 1,3-propanediol through microbial action. This is used to manufacture polypropylene terephthalate and Sorona® fabric. Researchers at DuPont engineered an organism for use in bioreactors that replaces some highly toxic petrochemical reagents. The biocatalytic production of 1,3-propanediol comes from renewable resources such as corn and offers material health as well as economic advantages. The Sorona® fabric, with its softness, good stretch and recovery, is in effect approximately half bio-based. The 1,3-propanediol is currently reacted with petroleum-based terephthalic acid to produce Sorona. While this may seem less than ideal (and it is), it represents a significant improvement over former practices throughout the lifecycle of the product. Also, the 1,3-propandiol may be used in other products and processes and may affect other supply chains.

Bayer Corporation and Bayer AG developed an environmentally friendly and readily biodegradable chelating agent, Baypure™ CX: Iminodisuccinate. Chelating agents are used in a variety of applications, including detergents used for cleaning textiles in industrial, institutional or household products; agricultural nutrients; and household and industrial cleaners. Traditionally, chelating agents biodegrade poorly and have high water solubility. They mobilize metals into the environment. Bayer's chelating agent is readily biodegradable, thus serving as a "nutrient" in a "biological metabolism" described by the "waste equals food" principle of Cradle to Cradle Design. According to Bayer, their sodium iminodisuccinate is also manufactured in a waste-free process.

NatureWorks LLC received their PGCC Award for the manufacture of polylactic acid (PLA) polymers derived entirely from annually renewable resources. PLA exhibits properties that allow it to compete with traditional fibers and plastic packaging materials on both a cost and performance basis. PLA fibers can bridge the gap between conventional synthetic fibers and natural fibers such as silk, wool, and cotton. Clothing made with NatureWorks® polymers has a unique combination of desirable attributes such as superior hand, touch, drape, wrinkle resistance, excellent moisture management and resilience.

Novozymes North America, Inc. won a PGCC award for their BioPreparation™ enzymatic process for cotton textiles. The preparation of cotton fiber, yarn, and fabric has environmentally damaging consequences. Approximately 40 billion pounds of cotton fiber are prepared annually on a global scale. Environmentally harsh chemicals have been used traditionally to remove cotton wax, which is a natural component in the outer layer of cotton fibers, in order to prepare the textile for dyeing and finishing. These processes typically involve treatment of the cotton substrate with hot solutions of sodium hydroxide, chelating agents, and surface-active agents, often followed by neutralization with acetic acid. Novozymes' BioPreparation technology offers a mild, enzymatic alternative to sodium hydroxide. Among its many advantages for textile wet processing are reduced biological and chemical oxygen demand on rivers, and decreased water use.

REMEMBER THE BIG PICTURE

Keeping the big picture in mind is important for many reasons. In the long run, we envision a world of sustainable materials where humans live and create and enjoy the fruits of their creativity, knowing that the matter we shape and move is being assimilated and integrated into living organisms and environmental and industrial ecosystems in ways that are benign and sustainable. Optimizing the material health of the textile industry through green chemistry holds enormous promise. With the support of visionary corporations and government-sponsored awards, chemists can design textiles that support life in all its diversity.

———∞———

Not Just Another Eco-Label: An Industry-Wide Solution

Peter Waeber, CEO

Luca Engel, Dipl. Ing. ETH
bluesign technologies ag

Lerchenfeldstrasse 5
9014 St.Gallen, Switzerland
www.bluesign.com

What Aristotle said in ancient times still holds true today: "Fine feathers make fine birds." Looking fashionable is such a preoccupation that it is easy to forget the other purpose of clothes: protecting us from the environment. Whether the item is a sweat- and odor-absorbent tennis dress, motorcycle gear, or a warm winter coat, consumers not only expect clothing to protect them from the environment, but also not to harm the environment.

Maintaining sustainability, functionality, quality and design will be crucial for future success. The companies that take action now will be ahead of the competition. For a company on the brink of reforming itself, however, the view can be vertiginous and intimidating. Which standards should be met? What is the most cost-efficient way to minimize environmental impact? Which technologies should be adopted or dropped?

While some companies have bravely started to answer these questions by spending the money to develop unique methods and criteria, it is clear to most (whether chemical producers, manufacturers or retailers) that a unifying standard can make the transition to sustainability easier and less costly.

Restricted Substance Lists (RSLs) are one way that brands often seek to self-regulate. Since brands are a public focus, they protect themselves with RSLs to make sure there's a low amount of a harmful substance in their products. With regard to both efficient business practice and environmental protection, this technique is often counterproductive. An RSL itemizes harmful or dangerous substances and their maximum allowed concentration in textile consumer goods. Producing textiles industrially without the use of chemicals, some of which may be potentially dangerous, is unimaginable if not impossible. Brands have some control over the amount and type of chemicals they use. Even if they do not have any influence on the chemicals used during production, they can give the manufacturers RSLs to comply with. At first, self-regulation seems to be a great way to prove to consumers that a business respects the environment. But a closer look reveals several weaknesses.

Even at their most basic, RSLs hardly bring order and clear communication to a fractious industry. One might assume that RSLs tend to cover just the basic legislation and therefore resemble one another in important ways. Some RSLs do reiterate the laws, plain and simple. However, many companies use their RSLs to differentiate themselves from competitors. Therefore, it is in their interest to make theirs unique. International legislation can change on a daily basis and RSLs must change with them. Constantly adapting and amending increases the risk of working with an outdated list. Imagine being a manufacturer who tries to avoid non-compliance while serving dozens of different brands and retailers, each of whom has its own list RSL and list and laws. What a management headache!

The manufacturer also faces other challenges. A very detailed, comprehensive RSL might be crystal clear to the toxicologist or environmental chemist who wrote it, but the textile manufacturer responsible for implementation might find him- or herself unable to interpret. Increasing chances for confusion, the environmental experts who prepare these RSLs frequently know precious little about the textile production process and therefore don't consider the manufacturer's situation.

In addition, RSLs restrict or even prohibit certain chemicals in the final product. Yet the manufacturer generally has no information about the occurrence of these substances in the chemical formulations used during production. Phones ring off the hook in the product safety regulation departments of chemical corporations that supply ready-to-use preparations. Everyone wants to know what chemical ingredients go into their mixes. It turns out that answering such questions with regard to the end product is harder than just checking the recipe. A legally accurate answer may prove elusive because the concentration of a certain chemical greatly depends on the parameters of the application process. Even the best chemical formulation can leave unwanted traces if the process is not conducted properly.

Finally, most RSLs are limited to consumer safety and ignore environmental impact. A t-shirt on sale in New York that is free of harmful substances can represent an environmental disaster if its manufacture meant poisoning West African cotton fields with fertilizer or dumping chemicals into an Indian river during the dyeing process.

Clearly, RSLs create more problems than they solve. It is in the industry's interest to replace cumbersome and opaque lists with transparent, respected, and widely recognized standards that include environmental considerations.

Many such regulatory concepts have been invented, but most of them fail to account for the realities of manufacturing, therefore missing opportunities to transform businesses into environmentally conscious organizations. A successful standard must see the manufacturing process holistically from raw to finished product. Granted, this is often difficult to do in a complex, global system where the trend watcher is located in the U.S., the designer in Italy, the cotton producer in Uzbekistan, the chemical supplier in India, the spinning company, dye house, weaving company and finishing department in ... Nevertheless, ignoring this complexity undermines environmental credibility. What seems to be the best solution for one production step may lead to major environmental health and safety (EHS) problems farther down the line that would mean resource-intensive processes that further pollute the environment.

Overly idealistic environmental regulations often end up compromising a product's performance characteristics. This is particularly true for high-end textiles and the result is a lot of disappointed consumers. To be marketable, a sustainable textile cannot underperform compared to its conventionally manufactured counterpart.

This is not to say that any self-proclaimed environmental standard can afford to be soft on resource waste. Any standard that takes sustainability seriously needs to acknowledge that consuming fewer resources is as important as using fewer chemicals. How can a normal cotton shirt be sustainable if finishing it takes its weight in chemicals and up to 300 times that in water?

Above all, the concept needs to be practical and easy to apply at the manufacturing level; otherwise, it is bound to fail as many other concepts have before. With these objectives in mind, bluesign technologies ag developed the bluesign® standard, an industrial standard that is applicable to the whole supply chain and that addresses both consumer safety and the complete range of EHS issues. They are: air emissions, water emissions, occupational health and resource management.

The complete service of bluesign technologies ag includes a screening designed for textile manufacturers. This consists of a full factory audit, including the evaluation of all relevant chemical preparations and components and an extensive process analysis. We give companies a sound, detailed overview of their own EHS situation. The audit also allows for the identification of possible resource and cost-saving opportunities. The data is then analyzed and summarized in an extensive screening report that includes recommendations of chemicals as well as ways to improve processes.

During the assessment of chemical preparations called "homologation", an EHS specialist acquires extensive information about the composition and ecological impact of a given chemical product. The specialist works with information acquired directly from the chemical industry (typically a much more dependable and accurate source than the manufacturer). She then evaluates all commercially available preparations against EHS requirements derived from legislation and environmental regulations. (The latter, though useful and influential, may not be mandatory.) The bluesign® standard also gives some consideration to popular or "emotional" opinions about certain substances. Scientific research might show that, in a specific industrial context, a given chemical has a negligible environmental impact. However, if widespread public suspicion of this chemical could result in rejection of any product associated with it, then this chemical could have a harmful effect upon a brand's image.

The specialist translates her evaluation into a simple rating: blue, grey or black. In this context, a blue component complies with all EHS standards in common applications. Provided all manufacturing processes are conducted appropriately, a product manufactured with only blue chemical components is environmentally friendly and poses no risk to the workers during production, the consumer during use, or to human health under any conditions. One example of a blue component is a biodegradable washing agent that is not toxic to aquatic organisms, doesn't contain any VOCs, and does not threaten human health. Components with a black rating, such as products containing TBT (tributylin) are banned from the manufacturing process.

Components that do not fall into the blue or the black category are labeled grey. These chemicals meet all consumer safety requirements but exceed EHS limits. They are only admissible if processed with the best available technology. In automotive textiles, for example, light fastness ranks high among performance challenges. Metal complex dyes yield the best results. However, these dyes can harm aquatic organisms. Under the bluesign® standard, a plant would need to have the relevant wastewater treatment in order to use this kind of dyestuff.

Bluesign technologies ag always encourages the use of blue chemical components. At the same time, if a certain performance is needed or if no alternative blue component is available, grey components may be used provided that the company can guarantee compliance with all EHS requirements. Grey components in particular highlight the need to consider the processing technology. Some manufacturers have their own water treatment plants or very sophisticated air filter systems. These allow them to responsibly use grey-rated products. A factory without such technology could not use the same chemicals and still meet the bluesign® standard. It would have to replace either the chemicals or the machinery.

Once they have been color-coded, chemicals are entered into a constantly growing chemical products database that enables a textile manufacturer to quickly find solutions to chemical preparation selection, even if he has limited chemical knowledge. If, during assessment, a manufacturer discovers he is using many black components, he can simply refer to the database for alternatives.

Beyond the individual chemical components, blue-sign technologies ag takes into consideration the environmental impact and efficiency of the entire manufacturing process. Using strict controls, the current practices are analyzed and compared to the best available technology. The bluesign® standard encourages conserving resources such as water, energy and chemicals during the manufacturing process, a tactic that almost always conserves money. Based upon the cost-saving potential revealed by these tests, recommendations to update technology may be made. Cost-savings of several hundred thousand dollars per year are no exception. Calculations are affected by the current production method, the range of articles produced, and the size of the manufacturing plant.

To be influential and enduring, an environmental textiles standard can no more ignore the environment than industry realities or consumer needs. Bluesign technologies ag exemplifies a sophisticated approach that relies on scientific expertise and a system-oriented approach to make environmental reform as easy as possible without compromising functionality, quality or design. Chemical suppliers, textile manufacturers, and retailers, consumers, and most importantly, the environment benefit from this standard.

The Lotus Effect: Or How to Make a Self-Cleaning Suit

Dr. Philip J. Brown, Ph. D., Assistant Professor School of Materials Science and Engineering

Clemson University
Clemson, SC 29634

Chemical surface modifications on fibers are literally as "old as the hills," considering that evolutionary processes have been modifying plant and animal fibers for survival since the dawn of time. Humans have adapted this concept for textiles, developing finishing techniques to modify fibers to suit our own needs. Yet despite years of technological advances, our synthetic modifications are far from perfect. Looking over the textile research of the past 100 years, we find that the same problems and issues continually resurface. In 1905, Percy Bean published a rather extensive two-volume book on the chemistry and practice of textile finishing, in which he outlined concerns very similar to those we face today. Bean worked with cotton, linen and artificial silk fabrics (viscose) and examined ways to enhance the properties of his fabrics by making the fibers softer, anti-mildew, fireproof, waterproof or rotproof. Since then, advances in the fields of polymer science, fiber physics and organic chemistry have greatly expanded the range of solutions for these and other problems arising from the inherent properties of natural and synthetic fibers.

One might ask the question, what else is there to do? Certainly many of the basic issues—such as repellency, softness, anti-static, flame resistance, crease resistance, insect resistance, anti-microbial issues, etc.—have been solved (or nearly) in one way or another. Consequently, innovations today must solve not just the same age-old problems, but also enhance fiber and fabric functionalities beyond those expected by the everyday consumer. By adding new functionalities, manufacturers create fresh marketing opportunities and more ways to distinguish their brand.

The avant-garde chemical surface scientists and fiber modifiers of today find themselves revisiting "the hills" for inspiration, copying nature's tricks. This approach is called "biomimetics." By mimicking the somewhat unique functionalities found in plants, animals and insects, we are reinventing fibers and textiles.

One inspiration for surface scientists and textile chemists comes from the lotus leaf. The lotus leaf developed its remarkable ability to self-clean through an evolutionary process. The plant inhabits a muddy, swamp-like environment and survives through photosynthesis, which necessitates a way to keep its leaves clean. The properties of the lotus leaves are termed ultrahydrophobic, super-repellent and self-cleaning. A number of years ago, botanists discovered that the secret to these unique properties lay in the fine surface structure of the lotus leaves. When examined under an electron microscope, the lotus leaf surface is extensively occupied by tiny bumps. The bumps are a couple of microns in diameter (2/1 million meters) at their base and taper to a sharp point. When a water droplet lands on the leaf surface, it essentially balances on the spiky tips of the bumps, forming an almost perfect sphere. Then it rolls off. In doing so, the droplet collects any dirt in its path and washes it away. The observed magnitude of this effect is startling. When the real-time event is slowed down via high-speed photography, the effect is simply breathtaking.

Here's an analogy to visualize the effect on a larger scale. Imagine that one morning you decide to walk out on your deck. The night before, a prankster stuck metal spikes onto the flooring. The bases of the spikes are one centimeter in diameter and taper to a sharp tip at one and a half centimeters high. They are glued all over the deck one centimeter apart. Unfortunately you are awestruck by the beautiful daybreak and neglect to look at the deck's surface before walking out in bare feet. Ouch! The spikiness is pretty repellent; you would probably jump off the deck.

After discovering the cause of the lotus effect, a question arose: Would it be possible to make a fiber with a similar surface? I initially heard this idea from an industrial collaborator who had published a paper on the effect in the early 1990s. At that time I didn't think it was possible to create such a surface given the technology available. In any case, no one seemed interested. Water-repellent technologies were available from a number of companies using fluorocarbons (a persistent organic pollutant) and silicones.

However, the idea intrigued me and remained at the back of my mind. Shortly after I arrived as a new faculty member in the School of Materials Science and Engineering at Clemson, I started to collaborate with my colleague, Dr. Igor Luzinov, who has a background in surface modification. At the time, we were bouncing ideas around for research proposals (our offices were three feet apart), and I pulled up the idea of the lotus effect. We decided to look into it. One of Igor's interests lies in applying thin nanolayer polymer coatings to materials in order to change their surface properties. At that time he had just made a remarkable discovery. He had found a polymer (long chain molecule) that could bind to almost any surface permanently, including glass, metals, polymers and therefore fibers. This layer is made up of polyglycidylmethacrylate (PGMA). Once bonded to a surface it can react with other materials such as other polymers or particles. This was the starting point. Looking back, it all seems terribly simple. All we had to do was bond a thin nanolayer of PGMA, and then firmly attach nanoparticles to the layer, and then react a final water repellent (hydrophobic) polymer layer over the top. ANY FIBER + COATING 1 + BUMPS + COATING 2 = CLEAN CLOTHES!

So the question then became, "Where are we going to get nanoparticles?" We enlisted the help of Dr. George Chumanov in the chemistry department. George makes nanoparticles of many different types, but his favorite is silver. The idea was getting even better. Not only would silver provide the bumps, but it would also contribute inherent anti-microbial action to the system. ANY FIBER + COATING 1 + SILVER BUMPS + COATING 2 = CLEAN, BUG-FREE CLOTHES!!

Since then it has been shown that this process can be applied to many fibers as well as to other materials substrates, such as glass and metals. In each case, the coating permanently bonds at a molecular level to the substrate. When applied to fibers, the handle of the resulting textile (to my touch, at least) is identical to that of the uncoated equivalent textile. As an added bonus, the lotus coating offers enhanced waterproof capability. It is suitable for all types of apparel, from socks to jackets to trousers.

Some practical concerns surround the processing procedure, which, though elegant, is also delicate. Poor execution could negatively affect the success of the coating. For example, prior to treatment, both the fabric's surface and the application machinery must be spotless. While this challenge is fairly easily overcome in a research environment such as a university, industrially, things might not be so simple. On the other hand, while the cost of silver may seem prohibitive, trials with cheaper particles, such as calcium carbonate, have been successful. With impetus shifting toward sustainable fibers, materials and renewable resources, the use of ultrahydrophobicity and self-cleaning materials raises a few questions. First, can you apply it to fibers made from renewable resources (i.e., those which are considered to be renewable through natural processes)? The answer is, yes. The coating can be applied to cotton, wool, silk and fibers made from corn-based resources such as polylactic acid. The issue then becomes, will the coating therefore have any effect on the degradation and composting of renewable textiles? In short, the honest answer is, I do not know. The ultrahydrophobic layer is not biodegradable. However, it is extremely thin—some 10,000 to 20,000 times thinner than typical textile fibers—so the amount of coating in the waste stream would be practically negligible. It is possible that the coating might decrease the degradation rate of the underlying material, but cutting or grinding the textile to expose the substrate, for example, might mitigate this effect.

A major advantage to this coating is its potential role in resource conservation. Most obviously, it represents an improvement over similar, existing coatings in that it requires less polymer mass to get the repellent effects typically seen with silicones or fluorocarbons. Moreover, it is also possible that, by decreasing or even obviating the need for detergents, ultrahydrophobic materials could reduce energy costs associated with washing. Widespread use of this coating would also encourage the development and proliferation of cutting-edge, detergent-free washing machines, such as those recently developed in Japan, which clean by way of ultrasonic energy or electrolysis. Such advanced technologies go hand in hand with self-cleaning coatings, because detergent prevents water from beading, thus negating the lotus effect. For very little material cost, ultrahydrophobic coatings could help our clothes look better for longer, as well as help us save water.

———— ✸ ————

SECTION 6:

BUSINESS CONSIDERS THE BIG PICTURE

Selling Eco-Fashion on Main Street

Summer Rayne Oakes, Model & Media Host
SRO

919 3rd Avenue, 39th Floor
New York, NY 10022 .
www.summerrayne.net

Several years ago, I assisted with Organic Portraits, a series of images taken by photographer John F. Cooper and photo stylist Peter Brown to raise money for women's weaving cooperatives and the conservation of the Chiapas rainforest. As a student at Cornell, I already had a strong environmental commitment because of my research on identifying toxins in sewage, monitoring stream water quality through biotic indexes and mapping invasive species with Geographic Information Systems. I also modeled, which I always thought of as a way to inform audiences of my "less glamorous," but far more important, environmental work. Working on Organic Portraits opened my eyes to the opportunity to bring sustainability and style together. From modeling to marketing, advocacy to outreach, branding to consulting, production to publicity, I've had the good fortune to be involved in an industry that is relatively young.

Unlike the organic foods industry, which has really taken off, sustainable fashion has yet to hit the mainstream. Whole Foods, the popular organic and natural foods retailer, became a Fortune 500 company in 2005. Sustainable fashion can boast no such equivalent; it doesn't even have a household name associated with it. Its prices, retail locations and raison d'être remain unreachable for the average consumer. Making sustainable fashion mainstream will entail making the products and concepts accessible and appealing to the consumer.

The latest Worldpanel Fashion Report, from market information company TNS, shows that 58 percent of British people under 25 don't care how their clothes are produced and only 14 percent of the 7,000 surveyed felt the use of organic materials in clothes was a "very important" purchasing consideration. Education about how apparel gets made and how that process can ravage human health and the world's resources would surely improve those statistics. For grades K-12, I put together a curriculum of 13 lessons about sustainable fashion that can be integrated into traditional school subjects. The pilot program was launched in September last year in Philadelphia public schools. Through lectures to professionals and students, I hope to spur the next generation of design students to think about sustainable practices and principles. To their credit, more and more American fashion design schools, like California College of the Arts, the Art Institute, Fashion Institute of Technology and Cornell University, are making efforts to inform their students about the effects of their design decisions.

However, people aren't always rational, and the dissemination of hard facts, while imperative, is not sufficient. We make buying decisions based on convenience, price, desire and cultural associations. At present, conventional fashion trumps sustainable fashion on all counts. This is to be expected; the "establishment" always benefits from superior financial and networking abilities. This certainly doesn't preclude sustainability becoming a force on the fashion scene, however. We should take stock of where sustainable fashion is, in terms of retail and marketing, in order to plan how it should advance.

The sustainable fashion community is diverse. In part, this is the natural consequence of sustainable fashion's neonatal stage of development. Its novelty has opened doors to talented independent designers who want to practice their ethics and stake their place in a crowded industry. It would be cynical, churlish even, to suggest that small designers adopt sustainability issues merely to differentiate themselves from the pack. Being "eco" is not enough to make bad design appetizing, but, in conjunction with good design, it is enough of a selling point to make early adopters take notice. In 2001, there were only a handful of eco-designers, but since then hundreds have staked their claim.

Forward-thinking designers are defining what sustainability means. Because the term "sustainability" refers to an end rather than a means, different companies focus on different strategies: organic fibers, fair trade labor standards, local design, handmade products, or clever chemistry. Of course, the abundance of techniques amounts to more opportunities for differentiation; but also, it lets companies choose a genuinely positive approach that complements their business model. The potential downside is that it might be confusing to customers. People who want to buy conscientiously may become discouraged if the "right way" is not clear. In a few years, consumers will become more familiar with the terms and issues, and it's hoped that the industry will be have meaningful certification to clarify a product's environmental impact.

While indie designers do not have the budgets for extravagant marketing campaigns and main-street storefronts, it's a testament to their power that they're exerting considerable influence over the fashion world from the bottom up. Traditionally, we think of trends as trickling down from big-name fashion houses. With the exception of Giorgio Armani and Stella McCartney, the iconic brands have chosen to remain aloof from hands-dirtying sustainability issues, preferring a l'art pour l'art philosophy. This is a shame, because sustainable fashion is not a trend or a look—it affects the entire business model. I predict that its values will color our concept of luxury.

While eco-designers do not yet appear on a monthly basis in the Vogues and the Elles, as a group they have caught the attention of some big names (notably Levi's, Nike, Wal-Mart), which are beginning to turn their huge ships onto an ethical course. Although it's easy to criticize such corporations for being too slow, they have many reasons to be cautious. They may be afraid of pushing the environmental message too hard because it will only apply to a fraction of their stock and reflect poorly on the rest (as if the rest came from sweatshops and was doused in formaldehyde). Or they may be wary of lawsuits. Retailers depend on their relationships with chemical and manufacturing companies. If companies were to band together and declare tomorrow that they would eschew azote dyes, say, they would risk being accused of possible collusion. Instead, to initiate change, many companies have to rely, for example, on educational workshops for their manufacturers. Although we may have to wait a few more years, corporate participation is necessary for the success of sustainable fashion. Indie designers simply aren't positioned to reach millions of consumers. They are largely dependent on the Internet to sell their wares and get their names out.

The best place to shop for eco-fashion is still online, either through the designer's own Web site or though green online boutiques, yet that "best" only attracts a small portion of total purchases. Although clothes sell well on the Internet (they dominate the category of small ticket items), online apparel sales are only a footnote of total apparel sales. The majority of online apparel sales are by large retailers that have brick-and-mortar stores. Independent designers who figure out how to set up their own shops will reach a much larger customer base. There is no denying, however, that the Internet has played a huge role in the sustainable design movement. But it can't supplant good old-fashioned floor space. Consumers who shop for the experience of shopping will not buy online, nor will they pay $159 for the latest organic cotton skinny leg jean if they can't try it on.

Though it's encouraging that some forward-thinking boutiques (usually located in major metropolitan areas) have also provided a place for many eco-designers, this has not offered indie designers tremendous growth opportunities for several reasons. First, designers must sell their products to many boutiques if they want to cover costs. This proves challenging if the designer does not have an experienced, pavement-pounding sales rep. Second, due to limited space, boutiques can typically carry only a few pieces from each designer at a time. Third, many boutiques place small orders or sell clothes on commission, which puts additional strain on new designers.

The Internet and, in particular, bloggers, have also played a critical role in disseminating sustainable fashion news and trends. But we need to get past the Internet. Despite breakthrough issues of Vanity Fair and Elle, traditional fashion magazines barely acknowledge sustainable style. (Although progressive magazines, such as Nylon and New Zealand-based Lucire have begun dedicating editorial space to green products.) And print is just the tip of the iceberg. All media outlets need to be tapped. It is heartening to know that the television industry, with its finger on the pulse of a young, progressive audience, is exploring green-oriented DIY and style programming, something viewers will start to see this year.

Bringing more advanced eco-fashion labels into multiple retailing and media routes will mark a milestone. But with mainstream success will come less opportunity for independent labels to distinguish themselves through sustainability issues. Figuring out how to build brand loyalty will become a life-or-death preoccupation for small labels when well-known and affordable brands with economies of scale really hit the marketplace. That said, in an industry where retail consolidation is a basic survival instinct, an eco-label with a devoted following will probably be bought by a group. That does not necessarily spell doom for its principles. On the contrary, if we can draw a comparison from the food industry, we see that Ben and Jerry's has actually been able to deepen its commitment to fair trade since its purchase by Unilever. Similarly, L'Oreal has not compromised The Body Shop's values, or Liz Claiborne in the case of PrAna. In these cases, the buying company realizes that the essence of the merged business was green, and that could not be diluted without also dampening consumer enthusiasm.

So how do we get sustainable fashion into the most prominent retail and media outlets, and ultimately into the hands of ordinary consumers everywhere? Celebrity-endorsed consumer campaigns and apparel product placement on heavily-watched television shows would push the maturation of sustainable style brands. Apparel-buying in both Europe and the United States is heavily influenced by what actors and actresses are wearing on hit television shows and movies. Moreover, having a recognizable face in ads almost guarantees greater media attention. The (Product) RED initiative expertly uses celebrity to raise consumer awareness of AIDS in Africa.

Sustainable fashion brands should also look for partnerships with other popular good causes. It has become common practice for causes to sell products to support themselves. Ideally, good causes should be allied with good products. Pink t-shirts sold in support of breast cancer should be made of organic cotton and dyed benignly; otherwise, we are perpetuating cancer.

Whether it's women weaving in Chiapas or sustainable fashion, successful promotion hinges on the association of ideas with broadly accepted values: beauty, celebrity, and other respected or appealing concepts, groups or demographics. Sustainable fashion has reached a pivotal point: we've attracted a small but loyal consumer base and the attention of corporate giants. Now we need to keep momentum strong, bringing it from the mill to our closets.

Making the Right Choice Easy

Penelope Cooke, Founder & Owner
Equa

28 Camden Passage
Islington
London N1 8ED
www.equaclothing.com

The modern fashion industry changes so quickly that consumers must purchase almost constantly in order to keep up with it. Abundant choice at different prices allows people of all ages and income levels to adopt the latest look. While there are benefits to this (economic class, for instance, is no longer ascertainable at a glance), much of this "fast fashion" is made using unsustainable methods, in environments that would shock consumers in the developed world. Much of it also ends up in landfills or charity shops after only one season.

By definition, doing something sustainably entails doing it in a way that will not compromise the ability of future generations to do the same. Sustainable fashion ensures the integrity of the fashion production process. But that's not the whole story. Sustainable fashion is often described as ethical fashion, which can be confusing. Different people have different ethics. For instance, some value social equity over environmental equilibrium (or vice versa). Various criteria can be applied to measure progress towards either goal. Do you value living wages over banning child labor? Recycling over non-toxic dyes? At some point, you just have to identify what you care about and what you can reasonably do, and then act.

Equa, my London boutique, was born out of a desire to support fair trade. Strictly speaking, fair trade means that the small farmers, plantation workers or factory workers involved in the production of an item receive a wage that not only allows them to subsist, but that also leaves them some money left over for community development or environmental management. Most of our clothes are made in fair trade-certified co-operatives. We also support small designers who choose to have their collections made in small workshops or factories that are carefully monitored to ensure healthy and respectful work practices. Since we recognize that British craftspeople face their own considerable challenges in the face of foreign competition, we look for products from the U.K. textile industry. Equa's commitment to fair trade serves as a kind of ethical foundation that supports our other concerns. We also sell clothing made from hemp or organically grown cotton, collections that have been produced from factory floor cuttings, and collections that are suitable for vegetarians and vegans.

Having identified a great cause, the challenge is to draw shoppers to it. I found that the typical ethical consumer is a woman aged 28 to a stylish 60, with disposable income. This knowledge helped me determine my location for Equa: Camden Passage, a fashionable neighborhood in North London.

I also realized that the clothes' ethical footprint would not be enough to sell them in profitable quantities. From the outset, it was clear to me that Equa had to be a design-led ethical business. Rather than basic tees or yoga wear, I wanted to stock wonderful dresses, elegant coats, stylish jeans and accessories. The fact that our clothes are fair trade attracts only a small number of shoppers. The majority of our customers buy our clothes because they stand out from the typical cloned and mass-produced apparel. When deciding whether or not to include a certain line, we ask ourselves: Could the collection sell based on its design, and not just its ethical story?

Equa stocks collections from about 10 different designers. All of our fair trade labels must present us with documentation of their supply chains. This transparency assures us that everyone involved in the production process—from the farmers to the seamstresses and tailors—is given a fair opportunity to make a living. This includes a living wage, defined hours, overtime payment, and access to job benefits such as pensions, maternity leave and sick leave.

Beyond that, wherever possible we stock clothes made from organically grown fibers such as cotton, hemp and flax. Organic growing techniques limit the negative impact on the environment. They also tend to benefit farming communities, not only by improving health but also by reducing crippling debt to chemical and genetically modified (GM) seed companies. Lastly, we strive to stock high-quality product in terms of fabric and production, to ensure that clothing will stand the test of time and not be thrown away after one season.

I am sometimes frustrated when people say that our clothing is expensive or overpriced. We have all become spoiled for choice and too used to getting cheap, poorly made, mass-produced fashion. We have lost sight of the true cost of what we buy. Fair trade exists in opposition to the unfair practices that enable the low-low prices one finds on the High Street. In some U.K. supermarkets, you can buy jeans for $10.00. You will never find a fair-trade pair for that price. Low prices cannot be the goal of an ethical business, although I want to stress that our prices do not include a higher-than-standard markup.

While some of the factors that keep prices higher may dissipate as the market matures, others will not. For instance, it is not inconceivable that the price of organic cotton will fall in the near future, as demand grows and as companies (such as People Tree) who buy in bulk and commit to buying organic cotton before it has even been sown, help decrease the premium on organic cotton. Equa wants to emphasize the value of our clothes, to encourage the consumer to see them not as a throwaway commodity, but as something one keeps and cherishes.

It is almost impossible to be all things to all people, and when you claim to be an ethical clothing boutique, this can be expected of you. The great thing (or not) about being ethical is that you can never do enough. There is always something else to work towards. If and when ethical fashion becomes more mainstream, there will be other issues, something more for Equa to strive for. This might be quite an exhausting thought, but I personally think it is a worthwhile challenge. We have held firm to our original goal and focused on sustainable clothing that will sell to anyone, regardless of his or her ethical beliefs. In this way, we are able to continuously move closer to the sustainable ideal.

The Advantage of Starting Fresh

Mark Galbraith, Product Designer
Nau, Inc.

Portland, OR

In my previous job as product line director, I researched, designed and developed technical apparel for a long-time market leader in environmentally conscious practices: Patagonia. The Patagonia philosophy is to make the best possible product with the least harmful impact. Patagonia was one of the first large companies to eliminate PVCs and introduce organic cotton and recycled polyester. It also strove to do good in other ways, such as by giving money to environmental organizations.

Perhaps Patagonia's efforts are all the more impressive because the company was founded before most green technology and know-how was developed. As a result, the company has had to re-organize itself to meet its goals, and that process inevitably requires time, patience and compromise. It is difficult for an established company to make these types of radical changes without threatening its legacy, its products and, by extension, customer loyalty.

During my eight-year tenure at Patagonia, I realized it was impossible to perfect the sustainability profile of every product we offered. The technology that would allow us to replace all of our "bad" materials with "good" ones simply didn't exist. A black-or-white attitude toward sustainability would have necessitated the withdrawal of some product lines, inevitably alienating customers. I certainly wouldn't advocate that a well-meaning company should be zealous to the point of undercutting itself. Yet I was irresistibly tempted by the possibility of starting fresh in a business that prioritized sustainability from its inception, and that could immediately take advantage of the latest technology to produce high-quality, low-impact products.

In 2005, Eric Reynolds, co-founder of the outdoor company Marmot, approached me with a plan for a new outdoor company that would try to do everything I'd dreamed. Eric had been in the outdoor industry for a long time and felt disenchanted. The consolidation of brands and retailers had a "Wal-Mart" effect, with a handful of buyers controlling what the consumer could purchase. Eric felt that it was time for a shakeup of both the product and distribution strategy. He wanted to try something completely new and was ambitious enough to get top-quality people working on it.

That concept is the framework of Nau today: an apparel company that meets the outdoor clothing needs of people who live in an urban environment (as most people do). The clothing combines the latest in high-performance apparel technology with classic, well-fitting style. Most importantly, it takes advantage of the most sustainable materials and processes.

Needless to say, Eric's pitch compelled me to leave Patagonia to work for Nau. There, I joined a team of like-minded designers and businesspeople from the outdoor and sportswear industries (Nike, Adidas and Patagonia, among others). All shared a deep interest in sustainability. As veterans of the outdoor industry, we were well acquainted with its standards in terms of performance (which is generally extremely high) and appreciation of nature (which tends to feature prominently in marketing material, at least). What we were generally missing, we felt, were style and a concrete, rigorous sustainability profile. Of the two, achieving sustainability proved the greater challenge.

We began by identifying desirable performance characteristics—durability, comfort, weatherproofing, etc. Finding materials was the most intensive part of the planning process, especially for me as product designer. Certainly, the company developed a Restricted Substance List to keep out such harmful chemicals as PVC, heavy metal dyes and many finishing chemicals. However, the list addresses only a fraction of the issues surrounding a sustainable apparel line. Setting guidelines beyond the level of specific chemicals was a more complex and subtle process. We think that making sustainable decisions requires balancing many criteria, and frankly, we don't have a hard-and-fast rule for prioritizing our materials requirements.

That said, we avoid sourcing any non-renewable materials that are not made from recycled content, as well as materials that don't have a clear, responsible end-of-life strategy (recycling or composting). As a consequence of the latter principle, we do not blend fibers if blending prevents them from being composted or recycled—such as the case of organic cotton and recycled polyester.

For fibers from renewable resources, we consider cultivation or ranching issues. We use only organic cotton. For our corn-based fabrics, we have temporarily adopted an offset program to purchase non-genetically modified (GMO) corn while we move toward the eventual goal of using only certified organic feedstock. The program consists of calculating the weight of the corn needed for a season's-worth of fiber, and then purchasing that amount of non-GMO corn for the dextrose processing plant that supplies the dextrose for our Poly Lactic Acid (PLA), the biopolymer we use that is derived from corn. For wool, we are developing land use, animal treatment and processing criteria. Organic wool is not the single obvious choice for us because we feel that the organic standards only address a fraction of the issues, and there is also the problem of limited supply.

Our next step was to stick our heads out there and see what the market could offer. In certain cases, there is no sustainable option that meets outdoor performance criteria. Lycra, added for stretch, is one example. Many of the materials on the shelves of sustainable suppliers did not address our needs in terms of aesthetics or performance. To circumvent this problem, we worked with the R&D departments of the most innovative textile mills to develop entirely new fabrics, among them a corn-based PLA fiber, high-quality recycled polyester, and several fabrics that incorporated organic cotton. Out of about 28 fabrics, only two of them were bought off the shelf.

The mills were willing to go the extra mile for us in part because we had strong existing relationships with them. In addition, our agreement with the mills stipulated that the technology they developed with us could be transferred to any other company that wanted to use it. Nau is not trying to make proprietary claims, and our attitude contrasts sharply with typical business strategy. We believe that open-handedness is central to the idea of sustainability. I never understood the sense of trying to make the world a better place while at the same time preventing others from following your lead. The only type of information that we keep to ourselves might be a certain pattern or weave, so that our product retains its distinctive aesthetic look.

We feel satisfied with our textiles. Improving the sustainability of trimmings (zippers, snaps and buckles, etc.) has been the most difficult. At this time, we use nickel-free metal and look for metals made with recycled content. At this stage, metal fastenings are simply much more durable than any of the available alternatives made from a renewable material. We feel it is important that our products last a long time.

For every product, we are developing a sustainable end strategy to keep them out of landfills. Our goal is that products will be either recycled or composted, and we are working on take-back programs. Teijin, our Japanese polyester supplier, offers Ecocycle™, the best chemical recycling program that we have found for apparel. Their process allows polyester garments to be recycled into a new PET polymer that is virtually undistinguishable from virgin PET. This method allows for the widest reuse. We also rely on more mechanical PET recycling services that create fibers for end uses which are usually further down the recycling ladder.

The design of the product itself also enhances sustainability. Our designs ensure that our products last 10 years. All of our products can be maintained using low-impact washing procedures, and nothing we make requires dry cleaning. Aesthetically, we ensure that the shape, color and fit of our products are not easily datable to a certain season. In the interest of increasing longevity and attracting customers, we have also decided not to put logos on our products. I think we've all experienced wanting to buy a particular piece of clothing but ultimately walking away from it after noticing the huge logo blazoned on the front and back. The idea of sticking logos all over a person as though he or she was a NASCAR driver is old-fashioned, as is the idea that by wearing a certain brand the consumer becomes an authentic member of a particular crowd. We suspect that our customers are not so interested in becoming walking billboards. They want to personalize their garments as they see fit, and they will enjoy them all the more for their subtlety.

In addition to material and design, we are implementing enlightened business operations. We have hired a third-party auditor to examine the labor and environmental practices of the factories we contract. We restrict the difference between the highest and lowest salary paid to 12 times. We are anticipating that we will receive LEED (Leadership in Energy and Environmental Design) Silver certification for our Boulder store. Because there are many factors as yet unresolved regarding our retail stores (such as exact locations, signed leases, final design, cost projections, etc.), it is not yet entirely clear whether we will be in a position to achieve LEED certification for all of our stores. We're exploring every option to achieve this goal. We purchase renewable energy for all our stores and corporate offices, and offset carbon for all product shipping and corporate travel.

With up to a 20 percent price difference between identical sustainable and conventional items, our business model has to create a cost advantage. From the outset, Eric advocated adopting the direct-to-consumer retail model. This benefits the environment by limiting the extraneous shipping that occurs with the traditional, brick-and-mortar store model. It also improves our margin enough to remain competitive. Hopefully, as supplies of sustainable materials increase, the costs will come down.

Since Nau's inception in 2005, we have already noticed an encouraging attitude shift toward sustainability issues from suppliers, customers and other companies. A lot of technological innovation is happening on the supply side, as manufacturers recognize the value of the eco-conscious market. On the retail end, recycled content fabric mills who previously accepted exclusive contracts with apparel companies are starting to open up. In the future, I look forward to meeting new designers who have been educated in sustainability. The sustainability movement feeds on its own momentum. The more customers that buy these products, the more retailers stock them, the more suppliers increase the supply and range of styles available, which in turn makes customers more likely to buy them.

Good for Business, Good for the Environment

Coral Rose, Founder
Eco-Innovations

P.O. Box 8845
Fayetteville, AR 72703
www.e-Ecoinnovations.com

In 2004, as the ladies' apparel buyer for Sam's Club, the warehouse club division of Wal-Mart Stores Inc., I found myself responsible for the economic, environmental and social impact of more than five million pounds of toxic chemicals used each year in the production of our conventional cotton merchandise. Of course, my job description did not specify those responsibilities; my conscience held me to them. I had experienced too much tragedy related to pesticide use to ignore the threat it poses.

I became aware of the danger of pesticides in the 1970s and 1980s with the malathion helicopter sprayings in the L.A. basin. First our family dog fell victim to pesti-cide poisoning. He developed numerous cancerous tumors all over his small body and, a short time later, one of the best friends anyone could have was buried.

I began to think, "Yikes, if that happened to Pee-Wee, what will happen to us?" A decade later, my mother passed away from cancer. Then a neighbor. At the same time, another neighbor (who survived) became ill with cancer. About five years later, my father passed away, also of cancer.

Given my personal history, the adoption of an organic lifestyle came naturally. For most of my life, I have been a consumer of organic food and organic clothing. I am often asked, "If you don't eat it, why would you care if your t-shirt is organic?" I care because of how cotton is produced. It is one of the most heavily sprayed crops in the world. Many of the agents used to spray cotton were originally developed in World War II as nerve gases. By the way, indi-rectly, you do eat cotton. Its oil can probably be found in your favorite junk food, and its seed is fed to the poultry and livestock that we in turn eat, and to the dairy cattle whose milk we drink.

Fortunately, cotton hasn't always been dependent upon chemicals. They have only been applied to cot-ton (and other farm products) in the last 60 years or so. Organic cotton, which is cultivated without these dangerous agents, is a completely viable alternative to conventional cotton.

As a buyer for a mass-market retailer, I realized that by buying organic cotton instead of conventional cotton, my colleagues and I could improve the quality of life of millions of people. After that insight, how could I not do something?

My perseverance resulted in a success story for Sam's Club and provided Wal-Mart with crucial economic evidence that doing the environment good would be good for business. I began looking for a supplier of organic cotton in 2003. Just when I thought I'd exhausted all my contacts, a current supplier called and asked me if I was interested in organic cotton. I was thrilled.

I knew that the success of a test in organic cotton would depend on the desirability of the end product. Ladies' apparel happened to be the number one volume category of organic textiles, and also one of the fastest growing. Next, I looked for the number one category in ladies' wear: active wear. Where does organic cotton fit into activewear? My answer was easy: yoga wear. I understood that organic cotton wasn't about trend. It was a lifestyle choice. The kind of person who would value organic would also probably value the comfort and health associated with yoga. So I developed yoga pants and tops in a selection of pastel colors. They were priced at a similar point as their conventional cotton counterparts would have been. My decision was logical, and based upon years of experience. We sold over 190,000 units in ten weeks, a number that speaks for itself.

When the sets hit the floor, I visited stores in several states to observe consumer buying patterns. I wanted to gain a fuller sense of their reaction to this ground-breaking product. I noticed that the typical buyer would be attracted by the item—the style and color—and the price; then she'd notice how soft it was. Then, I'd hear, "Oh, it's organic!" Some of the consumers, ones who fit the profile of conscientious "Patagonia-type" consumers, also seemed more apt to buy multiples. Clearly, they recognized the value.

What I learned, and what I'd like to drive home, is that it's about the item. The average Sam's Club member purchases on impulse. When she finds the right item, she will buy it. When she realizes it is organic, it fuels her enthusiasm. Organic cotton is a great added value for the consumer, but what makes her put down her money is finding the right item.

Of course, the Sam's Club member is not necessarily the same person as, say, the Patagonia customer. I'm guessing that the latter is more likely to shop at Patagonia because she knows that it sells organic products. Over the past decade, Patagonia has built quite a reputation for being a destination for organic cotton. Sam's Club does not seek to cater to a niche textile market, and environmental issues do not guide the average member's shopping decisions. That said, as the yoga clothes showed, Sam's Club shoppers do appreciate the chance to buy organic.

The yoga sets let me demonstrate decisively that choosing organic cotton could help a mass-market retailer meet or even surpass its immediate sales goals while doing the environment right. If I had developed the wrong yoga set, then the story would stop there. As it turns out, those yoga sets changed how retailers now view the opportunity to offer organic cotton to their customers, and it did transform a niche market fiber into a mass market fiber seemingly overnight.

Several months after ordering the yoga sets but before they hit the floor, I met Andrew Fraser, Fabric Manager for International Merchandising at Wal-Mart. His job was to source fabrics and then persuade buyers to buy them. Together, we drafted a one-page vision. Our goal was to develop a new business model for organic cotton and other sustainable materials, one that engaged stakeholders in horizontal collaboration throughout the supply chain, beginning at the farm gate.

Just as we were preparing to present it at the first meeting, my yoga sets hit the floor and began outselling every other item. Perfect timing. Andrew and I were able to present our vision to the executive committee with the economic business case in hand. The sales figures proved that, for Sam's Club, organic cotton was more than just a good idea.

Andrew and I began assembling a team in earnest. We launched a grassroots movement in the company. We talked to everyone, sent e-mails and posted flyers. We also had a secret weapon: kitty litter. Andrew and his three children spent one weekend creating the invitations to our first meeting. They were small plastic bags filled with five ounces of kitty litter. The note attached read, "The kitty litter in this bag weighs 1/3 pound, the amount of chemical fertilizers and pesticides used to conventionally grow enough cotton for a single t-shirt. Think of how many t-shirts we sell in one year!" It really grabbed people's attention. Everybody who was on our team joined not because they had to, but because they wanted to. They realized how important this issue was.

As we built support internally, my subsequent organic cotton purchases were coming through. There was not one weak sale among them, a fact that pleasantly surprised some people. It didn't surprise me. As I liked to say, "it's just cotton!" By that, I certainly didn't mean to belittle a $334 billion industry. Rather, I meant that organic cotton could be manufactured into any piece of clothing that conventional cotton is manufactured into. If the item sells well in conventional cotton, why should we doubt that it would sell as well in organic cotton, assuming the price point is close to the same? My sales figures supported that reasoning.

I kept hammering home the message that what we were making organic affordable for everyone. This statement in particular has become a mantra for the organic movement at Wal-Mart. It was the success of the organic fiber at Sam's Club, as well as the success of the energy and fleet teams, that gave crucial support to Wal-Mart's corporate environmental initiative. Across departments, the Sam's Club's success story has served as an example to build enthusiasm for organic products.

One particularly gratifying consequence of the Sam's Club success story was that it burst the classic lifetime adoption stages model. This model uses four stages to represent consumer conversion to organic buying habits. The model predicts that consumers enter the organic market with dairy, making that a stage one purchase. Fiber is a stage four, the last product type predicted to be adopted. With the affordably priced attractive yoga sets, we coaxed many consumers to enter the market at stage four. This indicates that proponents of organic clothing should not feel as though they have to wait for consumers to sufficiently evolve to buy organic. Consumers are ready and willing, as long as the product is also appealing in the dimensions that the consumer typically cares about: style, quality, and price. As you can imagine, as soon as I knew my goods were selling, I was over in the food area, sharing my story. The fact that I'd achieved a stage-four success story gave my colleagues in the food department the boost of confidence they needed to make their own organic purchases.

Whether they're dealing in apparel or food, because of their sheer size, big box retailers are in a privileged position to make organic widely affordable. This is in part because of the relationship they can build with the farmers. One challenge for the organic cotton farmer is the fact that, unlike the conventional cotton farmer, he or she must plant a rotation crop in order to maintain soil health. Wal-Mart has transformed that handicap into an advantage. In many cases, it is able to offer a market for the rotation crop as well.

This affordability trickles down to the customer. Making organic affordable for consumers was one of my personal motivations. In 2004, I visited my daughters, who are both raising young families—one in California and the other in Arkansas. Shopping together, I noticed that neither of them purchased any organic products. When I asked why, they explained to me that, as many mothers find, they just could not afford to. Their situation saddened me and brought into focus the real benefit of big box retailers' going organic. The ability to purchase healthy products (healthy both for the consumer and for the individuals involved in their manufacture) should not be a privilege determined by income level. Buying organic has an ethical dimension. It is not just about benefiting you or me. It's about benefiting others. Many people ask me how the Wal-Mart/Sam's Club experience changed my life. I reply that it never was about changing my life! It has always been about improving the lives of countless farmers, their families and their communities. Buying organic supports cleaner water, soil, and air. preserving the integrity of our ecosystems, as well as protecting the health of our children and grandchildren.

I have found that one of the most effective ways to impress this philosophy onto the corporate team is to take as many of them as possible on a farm tour. In

2005, we took several Wal-Mart buyers and suppliers to tour organic cotton farms in California and Texas. The trip was important to me in many ways. When I stepped off a bus in the San Joaquin Valley and smelled freshly-cut alfalfa, it took me back 40 years to when I spent all my summers on my grandparents' 120-acre farm there. However, I found that the valley wasn't the same beautiful place where, since the age of two, I had wanted to spend all my free time. While I recognized the smell of the alfalfa, the air did not smell clean and sweet as it did in my memory. Since my childhood, the area has transitioned from family farms to agricultural corporations. Many days, the pesticides, herbicides and fertilizers swirling in the air make being outside almost unbearable. Alfalfa is not the culprit crop. Cotton cultivation and other agriculture are the reason why nearly 194 million pounds of chemicals were dumped in the State of California in 2005.

Together with my team, I watched as crop dusters sprayed the conventional cotton fields with chemicals to defoliate the leaves from the cotton plant. Then we visited an organic cotton field. Organically grown cotton uses a natural process occurring during a seasonal freeze for defoliation. The contrast between the two fields was clear. The conventional cotton was brown and lifeless; the organic cotton vibrant with leaves that were glossy and green. At lunch that day, we listened to a local doctor speak about treating her patients, primarily farm workers and their young children, who suffered from mild to life-threatening illnesses caused by the chemical spraying of agricultural fields.

Usually, a buyer or supplier would never step into a cotton field. They normally get involved at the yarn stage. However, all of those who participated said that they wished that their colleagues from every department in the company could have come along. Before they went on the tour, they were making decisions with the organic farming projects because of the corporate initiative. After the tour, they better understood the environmental and social repercussions of their purchasing decisions.

Though Wal-Mart has certainly been an important force for change in the area of organic cotton and environmental reform in general, many companies are realizing that considering environmental impact and social responsibility are as critical as (and, in the long run, inseparable from) economic growth. I founded Eco-Innovations to support companies in integrating sustainable value into their services, strategies and products. I am currently leading a task force of industry experts that are committed to moving the market forward. They are among the top innovators and leaders in this industry: Levi's, Patagonia, Timberland and others. This group's intention is to make truly sustainable garments a reality by 2008. There is much work to be done in ensuring the total integrity of a garment. Fortunately, there is also a great community of industry leaders who are working hard to make it happen, and I feel privileged to be a part of it all.

SECTION 7:

WHAT HAPPENS NEXT

Can Sustainability Stay the Distance?

John Mowbray, Editor
Ecotextile News

80 Featherstone Lane
Featherstone
Pontefract
West Yorkshire
WF7 6LR, UK
www.ecotextile.com

The issue of sustainability in textiles and apparel has climbed to the top of the agenda for many major apparel brands and retailers, driven by increased consumer awareness of this issue in Europe and the U.S. The involvement of these brands has had a broad and deep effect on the textile industry, growing new markets and changing the way many companies do business. But whether these changes become standard practice depends in part on the longevity of consumer enthusiasm, and in part on economic verities linked to resource management.

An important part of many brands' greening strategy has been choosing responsible fibers. Wal-Mart has already identified the use of organics in apparel and textiles as an area of change that will have implications for fiber, yarn and fabric suppliers to the world's biggest retailer. At the moment, Wal-Mart buys around seven million kilos of organic cotton from suppliers in Turkey and India. Though this is a tiny amount in terms of its total fiber use, it has lined up additional suppliers of organic cotton in China, Texas and elsewhere. Other retailers and brands are looking more closely at the organic cotton route. For example, Nike recently stated that its goal is to blend a minimum of five percent organic cotton into all of its cotton materials by 2010, while expanding its offering of 100 percent certified organic cotton products. Patagonia, Timberland, Edun, H&M, Mountain Equipment Coop, Marks & Spencer and Coop Switzerland are all active in the market and expanding their programs.

The commitment of these retailers to organic cotton has transformed the industry. Currently, the world's supply of organic cotton is less than one and a half percent of the conventional cotton supply, but global organic cotton product sales have increased by an estimated 35 percent annually, from $245 million in 2001 to $583 million in 2005, and are projected to skyrocket to $2.6 billion by the end of 2008. Altogether, brands and retailers incorporated an estimated 9,066 metric tons (19,945,200 pounds or 42,552 bales) of organic cotton fiber into the products they offered to consumers in 2005.

Some synthetic fiber producers are also trying to muscle in on the sustainable scene. Perhaps the best established of the eco-conscious synthetic fibers is recycled polyester. Patagonia's "Ecospun" recycled fleece was developed in the early 1990s in partnership with Wellman fibers and Dyersburg fabrics. These companies used clear and green plastic bottles as raw material feedstock for the new recycled polyester apparel. The idea enjoyed some early success; however factors such as the relatively high price of the recycled fiber to virgin polyester, and its availability as only a short-staple spun yarn, meant that orders soon fell flat. Back then, consumers didn't grasp the significance of the recycled product and were unwilling to pay higher prices for it. As other brands proved slow on the uptake of the recycled concept, Wellman could not provide the economies of scale necessary to price Patagonia's fleece competitively. Since then, interest from apparel brands has grown along with consumer awareness, and there are a number of fiber producers offering recycled polyester yarns. Higher petroleum prices have pushed up the price of polyester, making recycled polyester relatively more affordable.

The green movement in fashion is creating new markets for both the most traditional and the most innovative of fibers. Wool now accounts for a tiny fraction of textile fiber usage, and the Australian Wool Growers Association believes that, by launching an "ethical wool" brand, it can create differentiation, lift low wool prices and stop industry attrition. All sectors of the growing, processing and manufacturing chain will benefit from the brand.

On the high-tech side, NatureWorks LLC, part of the Cargill Dow Group, offers a family of commercially available polymers derived from 100 percent annually renewable resources under the NatureWorks PLA (polylactide acid) and Ingeo fiber brands. The raw materials for Ingeo are fermented sugar extracted from corn and turned into pellets. The pellets are then extruded into filament yarns. However, Ingeo still supports the use of genetically engineered crops; hence, some organic purists such as Patagonia will not use the fiber.

A question on most apparel retailers' lips is, will consumer interest in sustainable textiles and apparel continue? In the fickle world of fashion, this season's trends are often consigned to the trash the following year. So although eco-labels may be cool right now, what will happen next year?

Some apparel industry observers argue strongly that "eco-textiles" may have been "in" at the height of the eco-debate in the 1980s, but they no longer appeal to today's trendy consumers. Nowadays, clothing must be colorfast, easy to wear, and of course fashionable and cheap—and need no ironing. There is no doubt that what attracts some customers is image—brand name, style and design—rather than product characteristics. Few people are concerned about how a product is made and where it comes from.

However, in 2006, TNS Worldpanel Fashion (a company which monitors clothing, footwear and accessories purchasing trends) released a survey revealing that, at least in the U.K., more than half of the population does value ethical fashion. "Ethical production" could mean many things. Seventy-six percent of people questioned felt that an end to child labor and sweatshops is a very important driver of ethical production, closely followed by offering producers a fair price (60 percent) and damage caused to the environment (50 percent). Fourteen percent felt the use of organic fabric was very important. It is understandable that shoppers should feel far more strongly about the fair treatment of people than about a relatively abstract concept like "organic." However, while TNS Worldpanel Fashion suggested that this figure "flies in the face of some fashion retailers' decision to focus heavily on organic ranges," perhaps we should applaud corporate leadership on an issue that is in fact often intimately related to farmers' health and quality of life. Moreover, since this is the first ethical trends survey from TNS Worldpanel Fashion, there are no comparative results from the recent past which detail the growth of consumer awareness for organic products. It is likely that five years ago, consumers would not have even registered organics as a concern.

The survey also suggested that 27 percent of consumers would pay more for ethically produced clothing. Fifty-three percent would choose ethical if they didn't have to pay more, indicating a need for shops to keep the prices of ethical clothing reasonable.

Such feedback shows that issues of sustainability are indeed here for the longterm. And although the demand for this type of apparel is still relatively small, its growth is being driven by legislation and the need for economic sustainability rather than short-term fashion trends.

Take Europe as an example. REACH is a new EU law, to be fully implemented in 2007. It is designed to protect human health and the environment from the unknown risk of chemicals within the EU. Article Six of this legislation requires importers of consumer articles (such as apparel) to register any chemical that is defined as dangerous and likely to be released in quantities greater than one ton. This would be difficult enough for European retailers when backed up by a REACH-compliant EU supply chain, but is likely to be almost impossible with non-EU supply chains, which are typical. Nevertheless, setting the bar high will certainly encourage better performance.

Despite reservations about the workability of such legislation, major European apparel retailers and brands do want to address consumer concerns. The clothing industry wants to avoid the recent consumer scares associated with dangerous chemicals in foods, building materials and fake drugs. Subsequently, bans on specific Azo dye structures are in place across the EU, and the use of PVC (polyvinyl chloride) and phthalates in garment panel printing have rightfully become hot topics.

Chemicals and dyestuff producers have often been labeled the "bad boys" of the textile industry, and rightfully so on many occasions. However, chemical production itself does not necessarily entail pollution and resource waste; rather, a lack of effective legislation at the local level, together with poor manufacturing practices downstream, has brought about most environmental damage. It will be critical to address these issues in Asia. That continent now produces about 42 percent of global dyestuffs and is expected to consume 45 percent of the world dyestuff market by 2008. Together the Western suppliers Dystar, Huntsman (formerly Ciba), BASF and Clariant—probably the four largest suppliers of dyes and chemicals to the global textile industry—they account for approximately half of overall dyestuff production, and they must operate under the relatively strict standards imposed by other countries, such as the U.S., and in the EU.

They all now have a range of environmentally conscious products and serious sustainability initiatives, for which the phrase "Product Stewardship" has been coined. Based on the idea that the chemical manufacturer's responsibility for the product does not end when the delivery truck leaves the factory gate, these words imply that the supplier will provide customers with information on the health, safety and environmental impacts of their products in terms of storage, use and disposal. This stance comes as a response to new legislation, successful campaigning by pressure groups, and perhaps just as importantly, pressure from large brands and retailers armed with extensive restrictive substance lists (RSL).

Dystar has come up with the "controlled coloration" concept which if carried out carefully, minimizes the impact of dyestuffs on the environment as well as offering improved productivity for the textile producer. If fabric dyers and textile manufacturers can see a real cost benefit to sustainable practices, then it's much easier to get them to change their ways.

Dyestuff manufacturers also have a large role to play because they can engineer how their dyes behave, control dyestuff quality and purity, recommend application processes and assess the environmental impact of their products before commercial release. For example, to design reactive dyes for reduced environmental impact, you must choose a careful selection of intermediates – no banned amines and minimum AOX (absorbable organically bound halogens). A high color yield is also important as high fixation multifunctional dyes will lead to reduced levels of color in the effluent. Dyes can be made that are suitable for ultra low liquor ratio dyeing machinery. This minimizes energy, water and chemical consumption, and dyestuff producers can advise on compatibility to ensure "right first time" dyeing to minimize wasteful shading additions or garment reprocessing.

Nevertheless, there are still many unacceptable chemicals in the textile industry. Not to mention the range of toxic pesticides used in the production of some natural fibers such as cotton and wool. It is heartening that some of the top retailers and brands recognize that the push towards sustainable practice is pretty much irreversible. In the last couple of years, a new group of major competitor companies has even started to work together on product chemistry, safety, and regulatory matters by sharing best practices in RSL management, information and experiences. The companies have formed a new working group, the AFIRM Group, whose membership includes Adidas, C&A Buying, the Gap, Hennes & Mauritz, Levi Strauss & Co., Marks & Spencer, Nike, Nordstrom, Puma, S.Oliver, Tesco and Timberland. These companies met most recently in Hong Kong in 2006. They intend to do so again in Shanghai in 2007, with the goal of sharing best practice initiatives, updating a "master" RSL and formulating a strategy for implementing REACH legislation.

Driven by such legislation and increased consumer awareness, the use of eco-textiles will continue to be a growing influence on apparel retailers and brands. The idea that aggressive litigators may also find themselves in a position to sue a retailer should a particular garment dye, for instance, become linked to consumer health problems, brings the issue into even sharper focus.

It's estimated that energy accounts for between 10 to 15 percent of total textile production costs. Given that world energy costs are rising due to higher consumption in emerging economies and the regional instability in the Middle East, the apparel industry needs to more tightly control these costs.

The Economist magazine recently reported that 60 percent of the energy converted in power generation is wasted, illustrating that the price of energy is high, both in terms of the actual cost to the consumer and the consequences of the climate change that generating power from fossil fuels causes. Even if a small proportion of this wasted heat could be converted to useful power, it would be a good thing for both the apparel supply chain and the consumer.

The sports apparel firm PrAna offers an effective model for responsible energy use, and it recently won a Green Power Leadership award from the U.S. Environmental Protection Agency. Since 2005, PrAna has offset the power of 250 of its retail locations in the U.S., 100 percent of its headquarters, and all of the homes of its full-time employees. For PrAna, offsetting entails supporting the generation of an equal amount of renewable energy by purchasing U.S. EPA approved Renewable Energy Certificates (also known as "RECs" or "Green Tags"). Throughout 2006, PrAna's Natural Power initiative offset 17,589 electrical megawatt hours, preventing the emission of 23,252,658 pounds of greenhouse gases—the equivalent of removing 2,283 cars from the road, planting 8,789 acres of trees, or converting 1,614 average U.S. homes to green energy for one year. In 2007, PrAna plans to increase the number of retailers participating, as well as offset a portion of its contracted U.S.-based manufacturing.

Water is another pressing global issue. We may be able to find and develop alternative energy sources, but we cannot manufacture any more water. The textile and apparel industry is a huge consumer of water, especially during the dyeing and finishing process. The threat of its thirstiness is immediately relevant to China. China's rapidly growing textile industry is consuming increasingly huge amounts of water in an environment where it is already scarce. According to the Chinese government, 40 percent of the population already lives on an amount of water considered below internationally acceptable levels. These people must compete for drinking water with textile, food and steel manufacture. Every ton of rice needs 2,000 tons of water to reach maturity. To produce one ton of steel, the backbone of China's new infrastructure, 20,000 gallons of freshwater are required. According to Huntsman, the Swiss-based supplier of textile dyes and chemicals, the production of just one kilo of cotton or wool consumes from 100 to 200 liters of water. There are the many extra thousands of gallons of water used for irrigation (cotton), and for scouring, degreasing and growing feed for wool fabric production. Last year, hot weather and a severe drought in China left more than 18 million people short of drinking water and damaged millions of hectares of cropland in the Sichuan basin in southwest China. As the global climate becomes more unpredictable, governments such as China's will seek greater control over water supplies, and how they are being used.

Hong Kong-based Esquel Group, one of the world's leading producers of cotton shirts, is taking the issue of sustainability very seriously. In April 2006, Esquel worked with the Zhejiang Institute of Science & Technology in China to establish the ZIST Esquel Eco-Textile Research Center (ZERC). The collaboration is expected to be the first of many joint initiatives between academia and private enterprise in China to foster scientific research on eco-textile production. It also sets a precedent for the promotion of research in textiles and ecology in China.

Consumers in the West will grow more aware as the issues of water and power availability become increasingly topical, and eventually impinge on the consumer's way of life. The very recent water supply problems experienced in China, along with other textile- and apparel-producing regions of the world such as India, show that it's likely that the production of sustainable textiles and apparel will increase in the future. In the long term, the movement towards eco-textiles may be driven neither by consumer awareness nor by apparel retailers wanting to promote their green credentials. Scarcity of water and the prohibitive cost of energy in certain regions may result in the sustainable production of textiles and apparel becoming an obligation—certainly not a passing fashion trend.

Not One But Many: New Visions for Fashion

Dr. Kate Fletcher, Sustainable Design Consultant in Fashion and Textiles

www.katefletcher.com

What links a merino wool t-shirt, a battered and bobbled Vivienne Westwood cardigan and a hand-me-down skinny black belt with heart-shaped studs? Answer: these are my favorite garments. Favorite not only because of how they look, but also because I know their material origins and makers, and I remember the people who gave them to me—and more than that, because they invite creative participation through personalizing and styling. My favorite garments encourage me to be engaged and connected, to be an active user of my clothes.

Achieving sustainable fashion will require more than just changing the way clothes are manufactured. It will require a new model of individual and social action that invites our participation with our clothes and, through them, with each other and the natural world. This involves a new approach to design, production and consumption. When people are seduced into being thoughtfully and actively engaged with what they wear—asking crucial questions like, Where does this come from? What are its possibilities now? What will happen to it next?—then sustainability will be within our grasp.

To effectively arbitrate the debate between environmentalists and the fashion industry, we must demonstrate clothing's potential to reflect aesthetic and ethical ideals. Both fashion and the environment are undeniably important. Yet it is often terribly frustrating to get proponents of either side to understand each other's position. To environmentalists, fashion is an unnecessary extravagance pandering to the vanity of the wealthy and contributing to escalating consumption. For the fashion sector, the moral imperative of sustainability threatens creativity and profit. Indeed, early attempts to forge common ground ran amok. "Eco-chic" in the 1990s, for example, was dominated by natural-looking colors and fibers that did not reflect real-world progress. All in all, the trend was more a stylized reaction against simplistic perceptions of chemicals and industrial pollution than a conversion to green values.

While the idea of sustainable fashion has matured in the past decade, as evidenced by the ethical fashion shows held in Paris, London and New York in 2006, a new vision must be created to counter the old view of sustainable fashion as a moralizing crusade led by the frugal and frumpy. We now see better conflict resolution tactics, but they generally constitute "tinkering around the edges" (e.g., tweaking dyeing and finishing standards, say, or by implementing green-oriented marketing strategies).

Companies investing in such approaches are contributing to change, and that is important, but they are not envisioning a radically different way of creating clothing. A new vision for fashion needs to fully acknowledge fashion's significance to human culture (as a medium for communication, a tool for empowerment, a fuel for creativity). This can be done by reconnecting us with the full range of possibilities and significations inherent in our clothes: their traditions, histories, materials and uses. We should also ask tough questions about consumption and personal satisfaction. The realization of this new vision will be a conscientious, sustainable, beautiful and entirely novel wardrobe.

To construct a healthier, more satisfying, more honest vision of fashion's future, we need design tools: tough, reliable concepts and models. Some of the most useful ones are suggested by our study of nature, especially diversity and the interconnectedness of things. Diversity is at the core of the future of sustainable fashion. In nature, diversity indicates the strength and resilience of ecosystems. In fashion, it means a wealth of ideas, potential and synergies.

At present, the fashion landscape is monolithic, dominated by a small number of similar garments and thematic trends. Though we may think of ourselves as spoiled for choice, most of the world's population swims in a sea of similarity. A lack of differentiation leads to boredom, which leads to over-consumption. It also erodes our sense of self. In contrast, diverse fashion, crafted by smaller makers, grows out of an individual or a particular place. The antithesis of generic, it favors expressiveness, difference and personal creativity, thus promoting the wearer's sense of self.

The vitality of ecosystems depends on relationships and on uses and exchanges of energy and resources. In the same way, the vitality of fashion's future will be secured in the relationships it fosters. We will see beauty and greatness in garments that value process, participation and social integration. We will also see this beauty in pieces that advance relationships between people and the environment: friends knitting together are beautiful, compostable garments are beautiful, supporting a disadvantaged community with careful purchasing is beautiful.

Relationships can be fostered by designing garments that encourage us to ask deep questions about our place in the world. Sustainable fashion forges a strong and nurturing relationship between consumer and producer. It is about producing garments that spark a debate, evoke a deep sense of meaning or require the user to "finish" them with skill, imagination or flair. It is about design confidence and capability, building pieces that encourage versatility, inventiveness, personalization and individual participation. When that happens, people will be transformed from blind consumers into active and competent citizens, making conscious choices as they buy, use and discard their clothes.

Applying future decisions to the physical reality of today's garments requires a major leap of imagination and creativity. Small signs of our readiness for this leap are all around us, in blogs, fashion magazine features, design school curricula, stock market sustainability reporting and corporate social responsibility initiatives. Launching this effort will require initiating a conversation about the sustainable future of fashion.

With that aim in mind, a small collaborative research project called Five Ways explores what sustainability qualities (i.e., diversity, participation, efficiency) might mean for fashion. Five Ways is a conceptual project producing prototypes and sketches rather than fully fledged, market-ready products. Its aim is not to prefigure the future or provide definitive answers to sustainability questions. Instead, it offers some ideas and promises starting points for investigating this complex and shifting territory.

Five Ways began with a team of designers and five simple briefs. From each of the briefs and associated workshop sessions, a prototype product was developed. While each of these products works individually, their real worth comes more from what they collectively represent: innovative outcomes based on sustainability values and a design approach that highlights interconnectedness. Five Ways explores things made around the corner from where you live, things that you never want to launder, things that work with human needs, things that have multiple lives pre-ordained, and things that require you to roll up your sleeves and get involved. Each of these five projects is described briefly below.

PROJECT 1: LOCAL

Where do you live? Where are your roots? The Local project captures the essence of your area and asks you to wear it proudly on your back. It asks you to find the world in your neighborhood and to know and support what's going on next door. Local products inspire and challenge the community, while at the same time creating jobs and making use of local resources. The "best" product is one with an energetic and material engagement with place.

In our case, local meant Brick Lane, London. Brick Lane has a very special character. It is the center of London's Bangladeshi community and a curry mecca. It has a street market, acts as a base for large numbers of designer/makers and artists, and is a thriving textile and leather area. Our product took these distinctive elements into consideration. We produced a bag hand-knitted by local workers from leather scraps gathered from local workshops. The bag is something in which to carry your fruit and vegetables home from the market stalls and it signals your community loyalties.

PROJECT 2: UPDATABLE

Trendy items capture a moment in time and are quickly cast aside. But what if that moment was not one but many moments, a process of transformation? What if that process required you to reach into the sewing kit and update that garment yourself? The Updatable project is all about a switch in emphasis from one garment to many garments, from passive consumers to active users, from a single snapshot to a movie.

Updatable involved a series of trend-savvy modifications to a t-shirt in an effort to keep it out of the dustbin for one more season. One half of the design team mailed instructions on how make the alterations to the other team members, who then interpreted the suggestions to produce a singularly stylish piece that they documented and wore over the next months.

PROJECT 3: NO WASH

No Wash took on the challenge of designing and wearing a garment that is never laundered. Washing clothes is a chore. Yet culturally and individually, we embrace it as fundamental to social acceptance, personal and romantic success and, ultimately, happiness. Keeping clean used to be about disease prevention, but now the West's obsession with hygiene has led to a point where the energy needed to wash a garment through its life span is about six times that needed to manufacture it.

In reaction, we designed a pullover partly to resist or repel dirt, but mainly to wear it like a badge. Developed in response to a six-month laundry diary, which documented most of the smell under the arms and the majority of dirt on cuffs, elbows and front panels, our garment featured wipe-clean surfaces and extra underarm ventilation. The pullover was worn for more than two years without washing. With its bold "decoration" of coffee spills and soap smells, No Wash reminds us of our garment's history as well as our responsibility.

PROJECT 4: NINE LIVES

Nine Lives draws attention to clothes' cat-like potential to die, only to live again. Although various forms of recycling—from second-hand stores to re-spun yarn to mattress stuffing—are always options for any old piece of apparel, the purpose of Nine Lives was to pre-ordain a specific reincarnation through design.

We produced two pieces, a knitted woolen top and a simple, printed A-line skirt, that were creatively morphed into one. Using the yarn carefully unwound from the top, and the sewing guide printed on the skirt, the owner stitches into the skirt to produce a new and unique piece. The unraveling of the jumper and the making of the new skirt are deliberate acts of creation that demonstrate a new way to engage with our garments.

PROJECT 5: SUPER SATISFIERS

Important uses of clothes include signaling who and what we are, attracting or repelling others and putting us in a particular frame of mind. These seemingly insatiable emotional needs often trigger dissatisfaction with ourselves and our clothes and determine what, how, and how much we buy.

What happens when our need for identity, affection and leisure are the explicit focus of a garment? Does this begin to break the chain of consumption and dissatisfaction? Does it focus our attention on the futility of trying to meet such emotional needs through clothing, or does the act of making hidden needs obvious connect us more with ourselves? For the Super Satisfiers project, we focused on the need for affection and developed the "caress dress," a highly personal take on attracting attention from others. The dress uses slits and subtle cut-aways to reveal hints of bare skin at the shoulder, the waist and the small of the back. Its purpose is to invite friends to touch you and to let you feel the warmth of others' affection.

What sustainable fashion needs is not a mass answer, but a mass of answers. While it has many limitations, Five Ways is an attempt to glimpse some of this diversity. Central to its success is its innovative design strategy, which emphasizes user/garment and person/environment interaction. Through insightful, practical and simple solutions, designers have the power to make consumers really care about what they wear. With caring will come change!

———oↄ⊃Ɛo———

The Persuasive Powers of Cool

Shalom Harlow
Fashion Model
❖

I was raised in a working-class city outside of Toronto. Even though we were not well off, like a lot of Canadian families at that time, we had a summer home. Summers were spent at the cottage on a small island in the Muskokas, surrounded by deep lake waters. The cabin that my great-grandfather built had no electricity or indoor plumbing. The forest was my playground, and I saw that the natural world around me was as alive as I was. I was taught to recognize that everything came from the earth and so must be cherished. Life here was rustic and I loved it.

At the time, fashion magazines were not something I was even aware existed. I got my clothes from second-hand stores long before vintage was cool. Because of my extra-long arms and legs, I was fortunate that my mother went to design school and could sew. Little did I know how fittings like these would become an integral part of my life. My mother's sewing sessions would be my only point of reference in a world that would soon seem drastically foreign to me.

At 16, I began modeling in Paris. I found myself in a world out of context from where I'd come, and antithetical to the way I had naively defined myself. I understood how Alice must have felt falling down the rabbit hole. How would I manage in a world where your shoes mattered more than who you were as a person? I couldn't help but think of the emperor's new clothes. It felt inconsistent that a skirt length could be considered revolutionary one year and embarrassing the next. I saw fashion as frivolous, and the endless consumption it promoted as wasteful. I questioned the sustainability of a hyper-trendy wardrobe that came with an expiration date.

However, I soon fell in love with the open-minded, free-thinking individuals and artists who abounded in this wonderfully wacky world. I enjoyed the grand theatrics of the shows. All the backstage drama reminded me of my dancing days. And I saw the gorgeous craftsmanship and the artistry of imagination that went into these couture creations.

Eventually, I began to recognize the impact designers have, not only on the world of high fashion, but on culture as a whole. They affect what we all wear. Even if you don't follow the latest runway trends, the trickle-down effect is far-reaching. Mainstream fashion companies import the shapes, lines, colors and fabrics from high-end designers, and funnel them into everyday clothes. Elements of a Yohji Yamamoto collection could be found a season later at Club Monaco. And so I began to recognize the pervasive power of a designer dress.

I was straddling two worlds. In one, I was a highly paid diva of the catwalk. In the other I was trying to be a regular teenager back home. It wasn't until some friends and I went to a rally where I was introduced to a book that chronicled the history of hemp that I understood the relationship of the environment to clothing. I discovered the potential healing effect the plant could have on the planet. I learned hemp could be a fabric, and required a fraction of the pesticides traditional cotton used. Then it struck me; clothes come from crops! This was a crucial realization. I had always understood the impact of food choices on the environment, but not of clothing choices. I began to connect the polka dots.

For the first time, I saw a way in which the two worlds of my reality could intersect. I realized that fashion could influence a future that was healthy and sustainable. The potential for a revolution within the business was a real epiphany for me. I envisioned a future closet filled with sustainable design, each article of clothing from a crop in which no chemical fertilizers or pesticides were used. The farmers who cultivated these crops would act as stewards for the land, fairly compensated for their efforts to protect a balanced ecosystem. Only natural dyes and centuries-old techniques worthy of revival would be used. The unseen human element in all that we wear would be honored, as each garment would be ethically manufactured. All this attention to detail and craftsmanship would lead to the longevity and durability of the garment.

In the last decade, many companies have made this vision of eco-chic a reality. Environmentally conscious fashionistas like myself now have an alternative to conventional clothing. Labels like John Patrick Organic, Stewart & Brown, Noir, Ceil, Anna Cohen and Linda Loudermilk are all harbingers of this new era of sustainable design. They are proving that alternative fabrics do not compromise the integrity of original and innovative design. Fibers like bamboo, sea cell, and Lyocell hold the promise of a future in which we can tread the planet gently. Companies like Patagonia have shown us that a global company can create consciously and consider the environment in each step of production. Now is the time for these practices and principles to be embraced and applied by other global brands. We must unite to support this new revolution of sustainable design. Businesses need to order the lines, stylists should include the pieces in magazine pages, and consumers must vote for the planet with the dollars they spend. The price point may be slightly higher at first, but the benefits far outweigh the cost to the earth and ultimately ourselves.

On a global scale, fashion has tremendous power to define the essence of hip. In an industry that prides itself on being forward-thinking, it seems obvious we should promote sustainable design. We can be the vanguard for a new era of sustainability. Let us use the persuasive powers of cool responsibly, to influence the way the world dresses each morning. Let us apply all our wisdom and technology to create a future in which we are guardians and beneficiaries of a precious planet.